Routledge Revivals

Social Structure

Originally published in 1942, during the Second World War and a time of great social and economic upheaval, Henry A. Mess endeavours to give a succinct account of the main elements in social structure and of their interrelations. He offers discussions on such broad topics as human nature, the role institutions play in society, and warfare as a universal feature of societies. This title is a short and accessible introduction to sociology and will be of value to students interested in the subject.

Social Structure

Henry A. Mess

Routledge
Taylor & Francis Group

First published in 1942
by George Allen & Unwin, Ltd.

This edition first published in 2016 by Routledge
2 Park Square, Milton Park, Abingdon, Oxon, OX14 4RN
and by Routledge
711 Third Avenue, New York, NY 10017

Routledge is an imprint of the Taylor & Francis Group, an informa business

© 1942 Henry A. Mess

All rights reserved. No part of this book may be reprinted or reproduced or utilised in any form or by any electronic, mechanical, or other means, now known or hereafter invented, including photocopying and recording, or in any information storage or retrieval system, without permission in writing from the publishers.

Publisher's Note
The publisher has gone to great lengths to ensure the quality of this reprint but points out that some imperfections in the original copies may be apparent.

Disclaimer
The publisher has made every effort to trace copyright holders and welcomes correspondence from those they have been unable to contact.

A Library of Congress record exists under LC control number: a 43000275

ISBN 13: 978-1-138-19166-2 (hbk)
ISBN 13: 978-1-315-64033-4 (ebk)
ISBN 13: 978-1-138-19173-0 (pbk)

SOCIAL STRUCTURE

by

Henry A. Mess
B.A., Ph.D.

Reader in Sociology in the
University of London

London
George Allen & Unwin Ltd.

First published in 1942

The Typography (and Binding) of this book conforms to
the Authorized Economy Standard.

All rights reserved

Printed in Great Britain by
Henderson & Spalding, London, W.1.

CONTENTS

	PAGE
PREFACE	6

CHAPTER

I.	THE NATURE OF SOCIETY	7
II.	THE BIOLOGICAL BASIS OF SOCIETY	14
III.	THE PSYCHOLOGICAL BASIS OF SOCIETY	31
IV.	PATTERNS OF BEHAVIOUR	39
V.	THE RÔLE OF IDEAS IN SOCIETY	57
VI.	SOCIAL HERITAGE	65
VII.	SOCIAL GROUPS	74
VIII.	GOVERNMENT	90
IX.	RELIGION AND THE CHURCHES	97
X.	EDUCATION	103
XI.	THE GEOGRAPHICAL SETTING	110
XII.	SUMMARY AND CONCLUSION	117
NAME INDEX		129
SUBJECT INDEX		130

PREFACE

I HAVE endeavoured to give succinctly an account of the main elements in social structure and of their interrelations. The subject is treated for the most part statically, and it is my intention to write in a later volume about the processes of social change.

No one can read or write much sociology without becoming aware of the present unsatisfactory state of its terminology, which is both deficient and also inconsistent in usage. I have made some innovations which I hope will commend themselves to my readers.

I wish to express my gratitude to Dr. H. B. Acton for very useful comments on the draft of Chapter V, and to Miss J. W. Armitage for assistance in proof-reading and in indexing.

H. A. M.

BEDFORD COLLEGE,
    March, 1942.

CHAPTER I

THE NATURE OF SOCIETY

WHEREVER there are men they are found to be living in societies. The simpler peoples, such as the Eskimos, or the Veddahs, or the Andaman Islanders, are commonly found in small groups, which may range in size from thirty or forty to a few hundred individuals. But for the most part human societies are larger than that. It is true that there may be found individuals who have lived with very little contact with other human beings; there are many well-authenticated stories of children who have been carried off and reared by wild animals; there are other well-authenticated stories of children reared in solitary confinement; and there are adults who become separated from their kind, castaways and prisoners and recluses. But such men and women are exceptional, and usually they appear to be damaged by solitude. In the case of those individuals who have been carried off in childhood there is always, for obvious reasons, defective development; to become a human being, in any adequate sense of that term, it is not sufficient to have been born of human stock, it is also necessary to have grown up in a human society and to have been subjected to its influences.

Those influences are of many kinds and of great power. The ordinary man does not, as a rule, realize the extent to which his thinking, his feeling, and his behaviour are likely to be social products. It seems to him that he thinks and that he feels as he does because it is natural and right to think and to feel in those ways, and that he behaves as he does because he has chosen so to behave. But a little reflection will show that most of us, indeed all of us, are to a large extent what we are because we belong to particular societies and to particular groups within those societies. It is obviously not fortuitous that most Arabs are Mohammedans, that most Cinghalese are Buddhists, that most Italians are Roman Catholics, that most Danes are Lutherans. The individual Arabs, Cinghalese, Italians, and Danes have not, with rare exceptions, thought out carefully the meaning of life and weighed the evidence for the truth or falsity of their own and other religions. If you or I had been Arabs or Danes, we should probably have been Mohammedans or Lutherans; it is the fact that we have been born and brought up in England, and not any reasoned and deliberate choice, which makes us non-Mohammedan and non-Lutheran. Even within this country the results of local group influence are observable; Methodists are plentiful in Cornwall but scarce in Scotland, whilst the reverse is true of Presbyterians. We do not conclude that most Cornishmen, on careful review of the evidence and arguments, prefer the dogmas and the polity of Methodism, and reject those of Presbyterianism, whilst Scots arrive in large numbers at opposite conclusions. We know perfectly well, when we take the trouble to think, that the majority of Cornishmen or of Scots are Methodists or Presbyterians by virtue of birth rather than by virtue of rational choice.

Or to take another example from the realm of politics: the facts about the War of 1914-1918 have been very differently perceived and interpreted by Britons, Frenchmen, Germans, Italians, and Americans. Germans, with few exceptions, took one view; Frenchmen, with few exceptions, took another view. Most Britons thought that the war was won mainly by the initial resistance on the Marne and by the pressure of the British Navy. Most Americans would say that American intervention saved the Allies. In Italian schools and in Italian history books the battle of Vittorio Veneto, scarcely known to most Englishmen, is looked upon as the turning point. Quite clearly, thought on the subject of that war is to a large extent a group product. Imagine an infant, let us say of neutral birth, adopted by a French family in 1900, or alternatively by a German family, he or she would pretty certainly think and feel differently to-day according to the land of adoption. Yet if he or she were unsophisticated, these thoughts and these feelings would seem to him or to her to result inevitably from the facts or from their consequences.

Again, within each social class there will be wide differences of intellect and of temperament and of experience, and these differences will tend to produce differences of outlook on many matters. But with regard to certain matters, such as in our own land and time, the control of industry and the division of the product of it, there is likely to be a fairly sharp contrast of views. Most members of the working classes will look at such questions in one way, and most members of the owning or managerial classes will look at them in another way. Those who live in Kensington do not for the most part think as do the majority of the inhabitants of Poplar; the people of Wigan and of Jarrow are likely to think otherwise than the people of Cheltenham and of Tunbridge Wells. Membership of a social class conditions much of our political thinking. And it influences our behaviour in many other spheres of life. We may think ourselves free to choose our partners in life, but actually our choice is considerably limited. Duke's son does not marry cook's daughter; King Cophetua and the Beggar Maid is prettier in ballad or in picture than in real life. And this restraint of social class is only one of the many restraints on free intermarriage.

In every society there is a climate of opinion: thoughts are entertained and actions are performed as a matter of course which in another society would be considered revolting. It is customary with quite a number of primitive peoples to abandon the old when they have become an intolerable burden, and this is not considered inhumane or incompatible with filial affection; in most civilized countries such behaviour would be considered monstrous. On the other hand our practice of waging warfare seems to some of the primitive peoples to be so horrible and so senseless as to be almost incredible. Decent men abandon their aged parents; decent men engage in warfare: their thinking and their behaviour are derived from ideas accepted in their society and absorbed, uncritically for the most part, by the individuals of each new generation.

It is obvious then, if once we have begun to think about it, that much of our thought and feeling and behaviour is a social product. We are moulded by pressures of which the majority of us are only dimly conscious. There are exceptions, certainly, or at least there are partial exceptions; some men and women stand apart from the general attitudes of their groups. But even the rebels are shaped in their thinking by that against which they rebel; no man escapes entirely the spirit of his age or the spirit of those groups of which he has been an intimate member; no man can order his behaviour, ignoring completely the social institutions of his society.

Much of this moulding of the individual is unrecognized by him, and much of it is exerted unconsciously by other members of the society. Modes of thought and of feeling are caught from one another and are passed on from generation to generation. We shall examine, in a later chapter, the tremendous force of custom. Social institutions, such as primogeniture, and systems, such as the feudal system, when once they have been established, may persist for a long time in a curiously impersonal way by their own momentum, and they may be very coercive. We are so used to them that we take them for granted, and we do not perceive how powerfully operative they are. It is one of the functions of the sociologist to bring into consciousness the social forces which commonly evade our notice.

But whilst much of this moulding of men by their fellows is unplanned, there is also much of it which is deliberate Societies have their ways of securing conformity of their members to the prevailing modes of thought and behaviour, and all the important groups within a society have their own means of doing so. Especially do societies operate in this regard through governments, churches, schools and colleges, and by the indefinite but potent pressure of public opinion.

Whilst men are moulded by the societies to which they belong, they are by no means merely passive and plastic. Human beings have, in supreme degree, that which is characteristic of all life; they react on and they modify their environments, and they select among the possibilities which are offered to them. They are shapers as well as shaped. We shall misunderstand human society if we think only of custom and not of initiative; we need to recognize the force exercised by leaders, by inventors, by pioneers of all kinds. An opposition between individual and society is sometimes formulated in terms which have no validity. A human life can only be lived in a network of relationships with other human lives, and it can only be understood when something is known of those relationships. But, equally, the term "society" is meaningless except as applied to a number of individuals and to the relationships in which they live with one another. And if what men are depends to a large extent upon the nature of the societies of which they are members, it is also true that what those societies are depends in the main upon the kind of individuals who are, and who have been, members of them.

Let us examine a little more closely what this means. We are conscious of differences between societies, we are conscious also that societies are subject to change. Of what nature are the differences and to what are they due? The broad outlines of the answer are not difficult to discern. In the first place there may be obvious racial differences between the peoples of these societies, and it seems likely that such differences will include congenital differences in mental make-up as well as differences in physical features. In the second place there are differences in customs, usages, and in social institutions, that is to say, in the kinds of behaviour which are normal, expected, encouraged, perhaps enforced, in those societies. And this means, of course, that they differ in the thoughts and feelings prevalent in them. Some part of the differences between societies is likely to be due to differences in geographical environment. And there will be much which can only be explained in the light of our knowledge of the history of any particular society; it is what it is because of contingencies, many of which were quite incalculable in advance.

It remains in this chapter to examine more closely what we mean by "society." With regard to this term, as with regard to many other terms in constant employment by sociologists, there is no agreed usage. Some sociologists define it so as to apply to collections of persons, others to relationships between persons, others to both persons and relationships. The definition which I propose covers both persons and relationships. I define a society as *a number of persons whose lives affect one another substantially, together with their relationships and their set modes of thought and behaviour.* It is with regard to the "substantially" that a second difficulty occurs, a difficulty reflected in the variety of definitions to be found. How substantially? Some sociologists demand "willed relationships"[1] between the members of a society; others ask for "mental interaction"[2]; whilst others again would apply the term "society" wherever there is interaction, even if it be unwilled and unrecognized.[3] The definition given above is in accord with the last of these views. But since it may be useful to have terms by which we can distinguish societies at different levels of integration, I propose to distinguish them as α-societies, β-societies, and γ-societies at the respective levels of mere interaction, mutual awareness, willed relationships.[4] Thus the Great Society of which Graham Wallas wrote was clearly an α-society, but an α-society likely to pass into the more integrated forms. Society in Durkheim's writings is nearly always a γ-society. The β-societies are not so easy to find, as they usually pass over fairly soon to become γ-societies, but some conurbations in this country are β-societies; towns formerly distinct and disjunct have been joined and interwoven; their inhabitants have partly realized what has happened; but organisation does not yet reflect what has happened. Many acute practical problems are due to the tardiness with which an α-society or a β-society passes on to become a γ-society.

---

[1] E.g., R. M. MacIver, "Community," p. 5.

[2] R. M. MacIver in his later book, "Society," p. 6. C. A. Ellwood specifies mutual awareness. "Introduction to Social Psychology," p. 7.

[3] E.g., M. Ginsberg, "Sociology," pp. 38-40.

[4] American sociologists recognize the different levels of integration by using the adjective "societal," as distinguished from merely "social." "*Societal*," *of or pertaining to society, especially organized society*."—*Webster's International Dictionary.*

FURTHER READING

C. A. Ellwood .. An Introduction to Social Psychology.
M. Ginsberg .. Sociology.
R. M. MacIver .. Society.
H. A. Mess .. On Terminology (*Sociological Review*, January, 1940).
Sumner and Keller The Science of Society. Vol. I.
Graham Wallas .. The Great Society.

CHAPTER II

THE BIOLOGICAL BASIS OF SOCIETY

WHAT any living creature is depends partly upon its original nature and partly upon the circumstances of its growth and life. Its original nature determines the range of its potentialities; but its subsequent history will decide which of these potentialities are realized and to what extent they are realized. The range of potentialities may be wide, but it has its strict limits which cannot be passed. Good or bad gardening, suitable or unsuitable soil, favourable or unfavourable weather, will elicit cabbages of very different qualities from seeds of the same kind; but if the seeds grow at all, they will develop into some kind of cabbage, never into turnips or into oak trees. And there are well-known different strains of cabbage. So it is with men. Generous nutrition, suitable surroundings, careful education, can do a good deal for a child born with dull brains, but they cannot make a genius of him, or even a good scholar. Adverse circumstances may frustrate the realization of the best possibilities inherent in an individual of good human stock; but they will not, unless they are overwhelming, prevent energy and ability from counting for a great deal in the struggle of life.

It is a matter of observation that like begets like. It is also obvious that like begets only partly like; the generations are not mere repetitions. And sometimes like seems to produce unlike, as when two brown-eyed human parents produce a child which remains blue eyed. Often traits skip one or more generations; sometimes they seem to disappear; sometimes a child will resemble a more distant relative rather than either of its parents. Whilst these and similar facts have been common knowledge for a long time past, the scientific study and explanation of them is a matter of considerably less than a century. Modern genetics is a development of discoveries made by the abbot Mendel in the 'sixties of the last century, discoveries whose significance was only partly perceived by himself, and by no one else for another thirty years.

Those who wish to study genetics must be referred to the text-books of that science; all that is appropriate to our purpose is to supply a brief summary of its principal findings, and to discuss the bearing of those findings upon our own subject, which is the study of human societies.

All higher forms of life are derived from the union of a male sperm and a female ovum, the resultant fertilized cell being, in the language of geneticists, an oosperm. Tiny in most creatures, microscopic in man, the composition of the oosperm determines in main outline the nature of the creature into which it will develop. The mechanism by which traits are transmitted down the generations is known, in part at least. If a germ cell be examined under the microscope at the stage of its development, when it is ripe for division and fusion, a number of small irregular rods or threads can be seen. To these the name of chromosomes has been given, and there is good reason to think that each chromosome contains a number of smaller units, which have been named genes. The genes are believed to contain material which produces the development of particular traits in individuals of the next generation. Whilst each gene is believed to be specially active in the determination of some special trait, it does not act alone; many other genes may contribute to determine the mode of its action; reciprocally it may be an effective, though minor, agent influencing the operation of other genes. Moreover, apart from the influence of genes upon genes, the development of traits from genes may be markedly different in different environments.

Chromosomes are in pairs in a normal living cell, one member of each pair being derived from each parent of that individual; but a germ cell, on ripening, splits into two cells and half of the chromosomes pass into each. Every germ cell ready for union contains, therefore, whether it be sperm or ovum, a half set of chromosomes. When sperm and ovum have coalesced, the resultant oosperm contains a full complement of pairs of chromosomes, each set being derived from two parents. These genes determine the characteristics of the developing new individual.

Knowledge of the mechanism of heredity throws light upon a number of observed phenomena of heredity, especially (*a*) inheritance of unit characters, (*b*) dominance and recessivity, (*c*) carriers, (*d*) linkage, (*e*) the non-transmission of acquired characters, (*f*) fluctuations and mutations.

Inheritance of Unit Characters. It was noted by Mendel that what an offspring receives from its parents is not a vague general resemblance to them, but a number of separate and sharply defined resemblances in detail. Thus Mendel, experimenting with pea plants, found that there could be passed on separately, and be re-combined in various ways, such traits as length of stem, shape of seeds, colour of seeds. Mendel was able to produce at will by suitable crossings :

Short stemmed plants with smooth skinned, yellow peas.
Short stemmed plants with wrinkled, yellow peas.
Short stemmed plants with smooth skinned, green peas.
Short stemmed plants with wrinkled, green peas.
Long stemmed plants with smooth skinned, yellow peas.
Long stemmed plants with wrinkled, yellow peas.
Long stemmed plants with smooth skinned, green peas.
Long stemmed plants with wrinkled, green peas.

And there were various other characters, such as position of flowers on the stem and colour of the unripe pod, which could be transmitted and could be combined by suitable fertilization.

The characters, it will be noted, did not blend. The stems of the offspring plants were *either* short or long, they were not of intermediate length; the seeds were *either* smooth skinned or wrinkled, they were not slightly wrinkled; their colour was *either* yellow or green, it was not greenish yellow. Similarly it is found by breeders that if horned and unhorned sheep are mated, the offspring are not sheep with rather short horns, but are either unhorned or have horns of the parental length. Differences between parental characters are not bridged; one or other of the characters is transmitted and appears.

Whilst it is highly probable that most inheritance is of unit characters, there is often an appearance of blending. The offspring of matings between white man and negro have skins of various colours, intermediate between white and black. In the same way eyes are to be found of colours intermediate between brown and blue. The explanation is that more than one character is involved in colour of skin or of eyes, and that some, but not all, of the pigments necessary to produce black skin or brown eyes may be present in the offspring of mixed stocks. It may be argued that this is in point of fact equivalent to a blending of parental characters, and for many practical purposes it is so; but knowledge of the unit character of inheritance is important in any attempt to predict or to control the appearance of future generations.

Dominance and Recessivity. When individuals of dissimilar stocks unite, the resultant fertilized cell will contain some pairs of dissimilar genes. But in respect of each unit character the offspring will resemble one parent only. It would appear, therefore, that one gene is operative, the other non-operative. Thus in man, if one parent comes of a pure stock of brown-eyed men and women, whilst the other parent comes of a pure stock of blue-eyed men and women, all the offspring of the first generation will be brown eyed. The character producing brownness of eye is said to be dominant, that producing blueness of eye is said to be recessive. For many living species lists of dominant and recessive characters can be drawn up. Thus in man, darkness of hair is dominant and fairness of hair is recessive; curliness of hair is dominant and straightness of hair is recessive; and there are other well-known pairs of dominants and recessives,[1] as well as many surmised pairs as to which the evidence is not conclusive.

Carriers. The recessive character is not, however, extinguished; the gene which might have produced it is

---

[1] For a list of such pairs of traits in man, see E. G. Conklin's "Heredity and Environment," or R. Ruggles Gates' "Heredity in Man."

transmitted, though its operation is inhibited by the presence of the dominant gene. The individuals of this first generation of cross fertilization exhibit only the character of the dominant gene, but they bear within themselves the recessive gene. And when they in turn become parents, when their pairs of chromosomes split in preparation for fertilization, half of the ripened germ cells will receive recessive genes. If such a ripened germ cell, containing a recessive gene, should encounter in fertilization another ripened germ cell, also containing the recessive gene for that particular character, there will be no dominant gene to prevent the offspring from exhibiting the recessive trait. In other words, individuals may transmit traits which they do not themselves exhibit. Thus two brown-eyed parents, if they are both of mixed stock, may have a blue-eyed child; two curly-haired parents may have a straight-haired child. Such a parent is said to be a "carrier" in respect of the trait which he or she does not exhibit. In the case of rare recessive traits, individuals exhibiting them may appear at long intervals.

Linkage. Since a number of genes are contained in a single chromosome, they naturally tend to pass over as a single group, though sometimes a chromosome breaks and its genes are divided. Also chromosomes which are close together in the germ cell are more likely to pass over together, when that cell is split in preparation for fertilization, than are chromosomes which are further apart. It follows from this that certain traits are likely to be found in combination, since they are produced by genes in the same chromosomes or in neighbouring chromosomes. Such traits are said to be *linked.* We all know that fairness of hair and blueness of eye commonly, though by no means always, go together; and that there are recognizable physical types, exhibiting groups of characteristics.

The Non-Inheritance of Acquired Characters. The developed body is derived from the original fertile cell by the division of that cell and the differentiations of the cells thus produced. But certain cells do not differentiate, and these become the germ cells from which the next generation is produced. These undifferentiated cells are little affected by the life history of the body into which the differentiated cells elaborate themselves. The qualities of an oosperm depend therefore upon the qualities of the original germinal material of the parents (and upon the fortuities of the processes of division and fusion), and little, if at all, upon the manner of life of those parents. To exemplify, if parents use their muscles much, their children will not therefore be more muscular; if parents use their brains little, they do not thereby impair the chances of their children being endowed with good brains. What is transmitted is the quality, or rather some of the qualities, of the original stocks. It is, however, true that some chemical agents and some physical agents may affect the germplasm either temporarily (which may mean over several generations) or permanently.

Fluctuations and Mutations. There are many small deviations from the mean in the products of a given stock in a more or less stereotyped environment, but these deviations are for the most part of small importance and tend to cancel out over a series of generations. There may be also from time to time sudden and considerable changes, which may be heritable; these are called mutations, and as to their causation there is as yet not much certain knowledge. Most mutations appear as recessive traits; and, to put it conversely, a large number of recessive traits appear to be nature's experiments, many of them unsuccessful experiments. But there are also valuable traits, such as musical ability, which appear to be recessives.

* * * *

The science of biology has already thrown a considerable amount of light upon the nature and the problems of human societies, and it will certainly throw a great deal more light upon them in the future. But the difficulties are great. The science is still comparatively young. Its application to man is far more difficult than its application to lower forms of life, partly because of the great complexity of the human organism and partly because experiments can seldom be made. It is particularly difficult to disentangle what is due to heredity from what is due to environment, the more so because human environments are very complicated and include psychic elements whose effects are not easily estimated. There is also the danger that emotional bias may vitiate interpretation. The possibilities of error are therefore many, and it is not surprising that there has been a good deal of rash dogmatization.

There is, however, a considerable body of well-tested knowledge about human heredity. There is no doubt that heredity plays a large part in determining such physical features as stature, build of body, leanness or obesity; pigmentation of eyes, hair, and skin. Many abnormalities of hands, feet, eyes, and teeth are transmitted hereditarily; and so also are tendencies to a number of diseases. Of far more importance to the study of society is the fact that quality of intelligence has a hereditary basis; and so have temperamental traits; and so have some special abilities.

* * * *

The mechanism of reproduction secures a continual supply of individuals, who result from the re-shuffling and re-combination of a large number of genes. The chances against exact repetition are enormous, and it may be assumed that each individual is unique in its inheritance. The one exception to this is the case of identical twins (more rarely triplets, quadruplets, quintuplets) where the individuals are derived from a single fertilized cell which has split at a very early stage of development. In such cases the inheritance is identical; but even then, slight differences in environment speedily cause some divergences in development. For all practical purposes we may take it that societies are composed of individuals, each of whom is unique. But since most societies consist of comparatively small intermarrying populations, these individuals are variations on a limited number of themes. Moreover, linkage secures that large numbers of them fall into fairly well-marked types. In most societies there is therefore a considerable measure of general likeness; there are to be found distinctive types, and each individual is unique.

A group of persons who, by reason of common ancestry, exhibit a number of distinctive traits, which are not found in that combination elsewhere, is said to be a *race*. Much labour has been devoted by scholars to the classification of the races of mankind. There is fairly good agreement as to the main races : Caucasian, Mongol, Negro, Australoid. The sub-division of the Caucasian race into Alpine, Mediterranean and Nordic races is generally accepted. But the classification of mankind into races is full of difficulties, and very different results are arrived at according to the criteria used. This is not surprising when one considers the many possible re-combinations of unit characters. Moreover, the traits which are commonly measured or estimated are subject to environmental influences. The one fact which has been established beyond cavil is that there have been mixtures of races from a very early period, so that considerable human populations of pure stock are seldom, if ever, to be found.

* * * *

Men, like all other living beings, are what they are in virtue of their environment as well as in virtue of their heredity; and their environment is complex and not always easy to apprehend. It consists in the first place of geographical factors such as climate, soil, and location ; and some indication of the importance of these is given in a later chapter.[1] Nutrition is of great importance : it affects stature, energy, resistance to disease, mental development, disposition ; the quantity, quality and suitability of nutrition depend partly upon geographical factors, partly upon level of technique and organization of the society, partly upon the status and competence of the individual. Environmental adjustments can sometimes be made to supplement or to correct deficiencies due to heredity ; thus we can supply spectacles to the hereditary myope, and we can give thyroid extract to the child whom nature has provided with a defective thyroid gland. Social organization and social atmosphere are important parts of human environment : what a man becomes, what a

---

[1] See Chapter XI.

group of men can be, depends in part upon the nature of the society into which they are born. In one society and at one time there will be *la carrière ouverte aux talents*, and the able man may go far ; in another society, or at another time, there will be rigid class distinctions and barriers which no ability can leap. Encouragement or discouragement play a big part in fostering or inhibiting mental development, as every wise teacher knows ; and social atmospheres may be favourable or unfavourable to the cultivation of certain kinds of ability. Ruth Benedict[1] and others have stressed the fact that a type of man for whom one society has little use or respect might be used and honoured in another society. In short, the nature of a society is environmental to its individual members and to any groups within it ; which is only expressing in other words what was said in the preceding chapter about the moulding of men by society.

The interaction of hereditary and of environmental factors is complex, and the attempt to assess their relative importance is difficult in the extreme. It is the more difficult in dealing with human affairs because of the bias which so often affects judgment. The socially successful, and members of dominant groups, tend to lay the stress on hereditary factors ; the less successful, and members of insurgent groups, tend to stress environmental factors. There have been long controversies with regard to the relative rôles of heredity and of environment in respect of races and of social classes. Many attempts have been made to describe the distinctive qualities of different races, and to explain national and regional differences of outlook in that manner. Thus distinctive temperaments have been attributed to Alpines, Mediterraneans, and Nordics. The inferiority of negroes to white men in intelligence has been asserted, and the non-emergence to date of negro nations and of negro states of any importance has been attributed to the congenital inability of negro populations to throw up leaders of outstanding personality.[2] It has been asserted

---

[1] Ruth Benedict, " Patterns of Culture " ; see also Margaret Mead, " Sex and Temperament in Three Primitive Societies."
[2] W. McDougall, " The Group Mind," Chapter VII.

roundly that some races are incapable of being civilized.[1] It may be so. But in view of the remarkable differences in outlook and in social institutions which are found between populations of closely allied stocks, and of the equally remarkable differences in the cultural life of the same peoples in different generations, there is good reason for scepticism. The argument from non-performance is particularly inconclusive; the ancestors of the civilized nations of to-day existed for many centuries in conditions of barbarism. We know very little about the conditions which favour outbursts of creative energy, or which bring them to an end. Nor do we know why creative energy takes some forms rather than others. The inhabitants of North America during the last hundred years have been of the same stocks as the inhabitants of Europe, and in some respects they have displayed at least as much energy and ability. But they have not produced many poets, painters, or musicians of very high rank, whilst in Europe a number of such have appeared in the same time. In this respect, at least, we suspect that the differences between the performances of the two populations, that of North America and that of Europe, are due to differences in social atmosphere and social tradition rather than to differences in hereditary endowments. It should make us cautious in arguing from performance or non-performance to ability.

There is no need to go to the other extreme of denying the reality and the importance of race differences. They certainly exist, and it is likely that differences in stock may account for some of the differences of cultures. But once we get away from the more patent facts of physique, it is not easy to substantiate assertion and speculation by convincing evidence. The alleged keenness of senses of many savage peoples seems to have no foundation in fact; and there do not seem to be any important differences in the sensory equipment of the various races.[2] In spite of many statements to the contrary, we know little for certain about differences in innate intelligence between the races. This is partly because, in many cases, it

---

[1] See M. A. de Gobineau, "Sur l'inégalité des races humaines," p. 75.
[2] T. R. Garth, "Race Psychology," p. 208.

is not possible to assign with confidence the individuals tested to any particular race, partly because it is not easy to say precisely what is meant by intelligence, and partly because it has not been found possible as yet to devise tests which eliminate environmental factors. There is some evidence, but it is by no means unequivocal, which suggests that the average intelligence of negroes is less than the average intelligence of white men; some evidence which suggests that the average intelligence of Chinese and Japanese is about the same as that of white men. When it comes to such matters as temperament, our knowledge is still less; the tests of temperament are very imperfect, and they are almost useless when applied to individuals of widely different cultural backgrounds.[1] Garth's provisional conclusion is that temperaments are fairly well distributed in all races.[2]

Our actual knowledge, therefore, of the innate potentialities of different races is small. The amount of dogmatic statement and of pseudo-scientific exposition is notoriously great. The sociologist should at present be wary of accepting such explanations, but he should not let his impatience with them blind him to the probability that genetic differences between races may account for some of the differences between societies. For the present he must be content to note the *a priori* likelihood and to wait for more definite knowledge until a more efficient technique has been devised and applied.

Similar, but smaller, difficulties attend the attempts to measure innate differences between social classes within the same nation. A good deal of information has been amassed in this country and in the United States of America by the use of intelligence tests, and again it should be realized that it is impossible to eliminate environmental factors. But, with this reservation, the evidence seems to point to two conclusions: (*a*) that, on the whole, the average of intelligence is slightly higher at the higher levels of the social scale; (*b*) that the range of differences of intelligence within a social

---
[1] See S. F. Nadel, "The Application of Intelligence Tests in the Anthropological Field," in "The Study of Society," edited F. C. Bartlett and others.
[2] T. R. Garth, "Race Psychology," p. 210.

class is far wider than the range of differences between the social classes. As to temperamental differences between the social classes we know next to nothing.

In the same way, it is hard to be certain how far the observed differences between the sexes are biologically determined and how far they are the result of social conditioning. Generalizations about the respective qualities of men and women have always abounded; it is only in recent decades that any attempt has been made to put them to scientific test. That men have on average greater muscular strength and are capable of more sustained physical effort seem to be established, and seem to be secondary sex characteristics. On the other hand the evidence is strong that women are more viable than men, more resistant to disease and to decay. That the sexual functions lay far heavier burdens on women than on men is obvious, and is inescapable, and to that extent they are handicapped heavily when they compete with men. There are slight differences in sensory equipment, but they are not of great social significance. Differences in innate intelligence appear to be small. It is very doubtful if women are dominated by their emotions to a greater extent than men. It has been asserted with considerable plausibility that great deviations from the norm are found less frequently among women than among men; in support of this thesis it is pointed out that both mentally defective persons and geniuses occur more rarely amongst women than amongst men. Certainly women have failed so far to reach the highest ranks in the great creative arts; there are no female counterparts of Dante, of Titian, of Beethoven. But, here again, to deduce from non-performance in the past is risky; it is difficult to assess sufficiently highly the depressing effects of the tradition of male superiority which has existed in most societies in most ages. What is certain is that there are real and inevitable differences between the sexes which are bound to affect their relations and their rôles in society, but that these differences have been exaggerated immensely and unnecessarily by social convention and by social tradition.

A cognate subject of inquiry, and subject of controversy,

has been the notable families which are to be found in this and other nations, families producing over several generations a number of men and women distinguished in some walk of life. Here again, it is possible to attribute the recurrence of distinguished individuals to the superiority of the stock. But it is also possible to lay stress on the importance of familial social heritage, the importance of a good start in life and the advantages of early familiarity with the personalities and with the techniques of various arts and professions, and to lay stress on the corresponding disadvantages of the *novus homo*. Once more, it is impossible in the present stage of knowledge to distinguish between what is due to favourable heredity and what is due to favourable environment. The same kind of question arises with regard to families of opposite nature, those which are prolific in defective individuals in generation after generation. With regard to them the recent tendency has been to consider that hereditary factors have been overstressed, environmental factors under-assessed.[1] The likelihood is that in both types of family both hereditary and environmental factors are part of the explanation. This is true also in all probability of the differences between the social classes. On the whole those who have good heredities are likely to obtain better environments than those who have bad heredities; on the whole the former will tend to rise in the social scale and the latter to fall in the social scale. They transmit to their offspring advantages both hereditary and environmental. Moreover, there is likely to be a measure of assortative mating, since men and women usually marry within their social class, and often marry those of similar type to themselves. There is therefore a process of social segregation tending to emphasize the character of the groups. But the complexities, both of biological development and of social structure, are too great for this process to be rapid or uniform. Theoretical considerations would lead us to expect some such result as the intelligence testing seems to indicate in the case of the social classes.

---

[1] See, for instance, L. T. Hogben's "Genetic Principles in Medicine and Social Science," p. 205.

The genetic composition of a population at any time depends upon the nature of the matings which have taken place in the past, especially in the recent past. These matings may be almost entirely within a small group; they may be almost entirely between persons of kindred stocks. Or many of them may occur between members of a very wide group, or across the borders of a group; and they may be between persons of widely different stocks. There may be, to express it shortly, inbreeding or outbreeding. Geographical isolation renders outbreeding rare and difficult. Strong religious sentiments, strong sentiments of social class, racial and national sentiments, strong cultural sentiments of many kinds, may check outbreeding; public opinion, ecclesiastical discipline, and laws may reinforce those sentiments. All these are capable of preventing any considerable amount of intermarriage between members of dissimilar groups. But even where strong sentiments exist, there is likely to be some clandestine mating if there are many occasions of propinquity; and wherever there is slavery, or any other form of strong domination of one social group over another social group, there is likely to be a good deal of mating outside of wedlock. All improvements in means of communication favour outbreeding; so also does the decay of the sentiments noted above. Very close inbreeding is usually checked by social rules, which may have the sanction of law, and which will almost certainly have the sanction of public opinion. Thus many primitive peoples have rules of exogamy. In Christendom, as in many other societies, there are degrees of affinity within which marriage is not allowed. And over almost the whole of the world there is a strong taboo against incest, though exceptions have been known, especially in the case of sacred royal families.

Some of the phenomena of inbreeding and of outbreeding have been observed from remote antiquity, but it is only since the formulation of the Mendelian theory that there has been a scientific explanation of them. Inbreeding assembles genes for recessive characters; it is therefore understandable that in small inbred populations a relatively high proportion of individuals are found exhibiting recessive traits. Since the majority of recessive traits are harmful, there is likely to be in such populations a high proportion of individuals with physical or mental defects. But some recessive traits are valuable, and since the genes for these are also assembled by inbreeding, a high proportion of individuals may be thrown up in an inbred population, exhibiting valuable traits. Indeed, it is not difficult to find small inbred groups of persons amongst whom exceptionally good qualities are found in association with conspicuous defects. Where stock is sound, inbreeding may continue over many generations without harm; but since few stocks are without some defects, the common opinion which condemns close inbreeding (e.g. cousin marriage) has much to commend it.

On the other hand extreme outbreeding is usually condemned by public opinion. There is evidence that in some cases, by no means in all cases, miscegenation does result in physical disharmonies;[1] it is possible, though this is speculative, that the children of such unions are endowed with disharmonious temperaments. But the greater part of the disharmonies and of the disadvantages in the lives of the offspring of mixed marriages are due to social causes rather than to biological causes; the children do not receive hearty recognition by the societies of either parent. Where social disapproval is not felt, the children of parents of widely different races are often successful individuals.

Genetic theory has thrown light upon a number of human problems. We have already a considerable body of well-tested knowledge as to the part played by heredity in the causation of disease, though much remains to be ascertained. It is generally recognized that hereditary factors are operative in a large proportion of cases of mental defect, though opinions differ widely as to the proportions and to the relative importance of hereditary and environmental factors. Some recent work on twins suggests strongly that similar, and still more identical, heredity plays a big part in predisposing individuals to similar anti-social behaviour.[2] It has also been suggested

---

[1] See, for instance, Miss Fleming's studies of the children of black-white parents in Liverpool, quoted by R. Ruggles Gates, "Heredity in Man," p. 356.
[2] See Johannes Lange, "Crime as Destiny."

with considerable plausibility that heredity plays a large part in producing individuals incapable of self-maintenance in our society.[1]

But in each class of cases the difficulties of disentangling hereditary factors from environmental factors are immense. It must be borne in mind steadily that what individuals are is only partly due to their heredity; their environments count enormously, and different environments will elicit very different results from the same stocks. It is quite conceivable that there may be proceeding concurrently in the society deterioration of stock together with improvement of environment, and that the result may be for a long time the maintenance of the quality of the individuals in that society. But, clearly, deterioration of stock is a very serious matter; and if it should go on unchecked, the time would come when the society was no longer capable of maintaining good environmental conditions.

By the provision of carefully adjusted environmental conditions much can be done to offset hereditary defects. Hereditary myopes can be provided with spectacles, special means of communication with their fellows can be devised for the deaf and dumb, persons of neuropathic stock can be guarded against undue strain, diabetics can be kept alive in reasonably good condition by a supply of insulin, those who inherit defective thyroid glands can be given thyroid extracts obtained from animals. Much modern scientific knowledge and scientific skill have been devoted to the task of correcting hereditary inadequacies by environmental adjustments.

But if the doctrine of the non-inheritance of acquired characters is true, as the majority of biologists believe it to be, it follows that no improvement of environment can improve stock. It may improve immensely what is obtained from that stock, but the stock remains unaffected and the next generation will start life with the same advantages and the same disadvantages as the previous generation. Environmental corrections must therefore be applied afresh in each generation.

---

[1] See E. J. Lidbetter, "Heredity and the Social Problem Group"; also D. Caradog Jones, "The Social Survey of Merseyside," Vol. III, pp. 546-47.

Improvement in stock might be effected by selective mating, and by the discouragement of individuals of defective stocks from breeding and corresponding encouragement of individuals of good stocks to breed freely; but such courses are full of grave difficulties, for the discussion of which the reader must be referred to the literature of eugenics.

In conclusion of this chapter, what a society is and how it differs from other societies depend in part, but in part only, upon its genetic composition. Similarly, changes in the nature of a society between one period and another period *may* be due to changes in genetic composition. But to determine with any precision how much is due to environmental forces and how much to genetic composition, is at present for the most part beyond the power of scientists.

FURTHER READING

ed. F. C. Bartlett	The Study of Society.
L. L. Bernard	Introduction to Social Psychology, Chapter VI.
E. G. Conklin	Heredity and Environment.
R. Ruggles Gates	Heredity in Man.
F. Herz	Race and Civilization.
J. Huxley and A. C. Haddon	We Europeans.
H. S. Jennings	The Biological Basis of Human Nature.
J. Lange	Crime as Destiny.
M. Mead	Sex and Temperament in Three Primitive Societies.
P. Sorokin	Contemporary Sociological Theories, Chapter V.
H. B. Thompson	The Mental Traits of Sex.

CHAPTER III

THE PSYCHOLOGICAL BASIS OF SOCIETY

It is beyond all doubt that there is hereditary transmission of specific psycho-physical tendencies: that is to say that men are so constituted that they are likely to behave in certain ways and not in other ways when they are confronted with certain types of situations. But as to what those tendencies are, how they will work out in behaviour, what is the range of possible expressions, to what extent they can be modified or inhibited, there has been, and still is, much controversy amongst psychologists. It is a matter of great difficulty to distinguish the innate from the acquired, what is due to heredity from what is due to environment.

The simplest and most definite of these tendencies are the reflexes, automatic responses to stimulation, such as the shutting of eyes in presence of a sudden flash of light, the watering of the mouth at the smell of food, the quickened breathing and the rapid beating of the heart in the presence of danger, the motion of a hand to touch an irritated part of the skin. We do not will these reflex processes, and while some of them can be inhibited or controlled, others cannot be; of some of them we are not even conscious.

Again, we have as part of our hereditary make-up the appetites, notably the appetites of hunger (in which may be included thirst) and sex. With regard to the former, we have considerable power of controlling the times and modes of satisfaction, but it will not be denied. With regard to the latter, we may proceed as far as complete inhibition. But both appetites are imperious and they are great driving forces in individual and in social life.

There are also to be observed in human beings tendencies of longer duration and issuing usually in behaviour of a more complicated kind. Men, for instance, exhibit pugnacity and curiosity; they assert themselves and they accept the lead of others; they are acquisitive, and often they exhibit an urge to construct something; they show a desire for one another's company. Such traits are not universal, and they vary in definiteness and in strength from individual to individual, and there are observable differences between societies in respect of them. With regard to these tendencies there has recently been a great shift of opinion. A few years ago they were commonly described by psychologists as instincts, and they were looked upon as being innate, though very plastic. To-day many psychologists are sceptical of the existence of such innate specific tendencies in man; they regard them as being developed by the circumstances of the individual's life out of the general urge of each individual to maintain itself, an urge which is of course innate. There are some psychologists who would even deny that there is any common human nature to be found in all men.[1] It is my opinion that, whilst the criticism has been very useful, the reaction against instinctivist doctrine has gone much too far. There are signs that the controversy is wearing itself out, and that a new middle position is being taken. Professor R. S. Woodworth, in the latest edition of his well-known text-book, "Psychology," dispenses with the word "instinct" on the ground of its ambiguity, and speaks of "learned and unlearned motives." Some part of maternal care, some fear, some pugnacity, some urge to manipulation, some urge to overcome resistance, he takes to be unlearned, i.e., innate; he is not so sure about gregariousness and submissiveness.[2] What is clear is that we have not as yet any well-established list of innate tendencies in men, nor any reliable means of measuring their strength; and that, whilst there is good reason for believing that such innate tendencies exist, we are not yet in a position in which

---

[1] "The age-old quest for a definitive list of traits common to humans as humans is a hopeless quest for constants which do not exist. . . . We shall clarify our thinking by throwing 'original human nature' to the limbo of past beliefs." J. F. Brown, "Psychology and the Social Order," p. 273.

[2] R. S. Woodworth, "Psychology," 12th edition, 1940, pp. 368-83

we can, with any confidence, argue deductively as to social behaviour.[1]

But in point of fact we can already make a number of useful statements about human nature as it is revealed in human behaviour. We can note in the first place some significant ways in which man stands apart from the lower animals. In the second place we can note a number of features which appear to be common to all human societies. In the third place we can note the diversities of behaviour to be found. And in the fourth place we can point to certain mechanisms of the human mind, modes in which it adapts itself to its experiences.

Of the differences between men and the lower animals there are two which are of outstanding importance for social development. Man possesses a vocal apparatus capable of producing a considerable number of distinct and clearly articulated sounds. And man possesses a brain capable of thinking in abstract terms. In virtue of these two capabilities men are able to communicate with one another more copiously and more precisely than the animals can do, and the gains of experience are more easily shared. They are able to build up language, and they are able at a later stage to express words by visual symbols. As a result of this they are able to pursue trains of reasoning, and they are able to store ideas. Easy and precise communication, the use of abstract ideas, and the storage of knowledge make possible social development.

When we come to consider what is common to all men (or to all men with so few exceptions that we may consider those exceptions to be abnormal) we find first of all that there are a number of statements which can be made of practically every human society of which we have knowledge. Everywhere men are found to be living in recognized relationships and following recognized patterns of behaviour. Everywhere there will be found some attempt to get in touch with unseen

---

[1] On the controversy with regard to instincts, see W. McDougall, "An Introduction to Social Psychology," and "The Energies of Men"; John Dewey, "Human Nature and Conduct"; P. Sorokin, "Contemporary Sociological Theories," pp. 603-17; M. Ginsberg, "Studies in Sociology, Chapter VII; and especially, as indicated above, R. S. Woodworth, "Psychology" (1940 edition), pp. 368-83.

powers which are conceived as being interested in and able to affect human welfare. Everywhere there will be found codes of morals, though the morals may be strangely different from those to which we are accustomed. Everywhere there is to be found authority and subordination, though sometimes ill defined. Everywhere there will be found conflict in some form, though the amount and the forms of it vary widely. Everywhere there will be found the institution of the family, though sometimes the family will take a form which seems very strange to us. Everywhere there is to be found some kind of economic co-operation. Everywhere there will be found, though it may be in a very restricted and rudimentary form, the sense of property. Everywhere men will be found to go beyond the necessities of life and to delight in activities for their own sake. Wherever men exist, they play; and wherever men exist, some kind of artistic expression is to be found.

We are justified in deducing from the universality of these phenomena that human nature is such that it is likely to issue in certain types of behaviour and in certain types of relationships. Can we say more, that it must so issue? We are given pause by the fact that there are other patterns of behaviour which are found usually but by no means always. Warfare is a conspicuous example. In view of its recurrence we might conclude that warfare issues inevitably from human nature (and indeed many persons do think so), if it were not well established that a considerable number of human societies are without it and apparently have never had it. We know also that slavery has sometimes seemed so pervasive that even wise men have concluded it to be a necessity of human society. Yet there have been many societies in the past which have not had slavery, and to-day it is not to be found in the great majority of societies. These instances make us hesitate if we are inclined to argue from what is and what has been to what must be. It is not certain that forms of behaviour which have been found always and everywhere in the past will of necessity be found in the future, though there is a strong presumption that it will be so. And we cannot argue with certainty from specific universal behaviour to specific innate drive, though again the presumption is considerable.

We have been stressing so far the uniformities in human behaviour, and these uniformities are very striking. But scarcely less striking is the variety of behaviours to be found. Any text-book of anthropology will bear witness to this, to the protean forms which the great social institutions such as marriage and property may assume, to the diverse manifestations of the emotions, of such emotions for instance as modesty and jealousy. And since great varieties of behaviour are to be found in societies whose members may be of the same, or closely allied, stock, we are bound to conclude that human nature is extremely plastic. What limits are there to its plasticity? It is a question of the greatest importance, but it is not one to which it is possible to give a satisfactory answer in the present state of knowledge. Obviously the controversy with regard to instincts is here of great relevance.

We turn now to consider some of the mechanisms of the human mind. In the first place there is the organization of thought and feeling into sentiments or complexes. A complex is defined by Hart as "a system of connected ideas, with a strong emotional tone and a tendency to produce actions of a certain definite type."[1] Thus patriotism is a sentiment, conjugal love is a sentiment. Many of our strongest sentiments are formed in childhood. Children find that those around them dislike foreigners, and there is built up in their own minds a body of thought and feeling inimical to foreigners. An inquiry a few years ago into the views of boys and girls in a number of Welsh schools showed that most children have formed racial prejudices by the time that they are seven years old. And once a strong sentiment has been formed it is very tenacious of existence and very resistant to change. Evidence which runs counter to it is usually rejected by the mind; evidence in support of it is sought and may be manufactured. Recent psychology has emphasized the fact, known to wise men for many centuries, that our emotions often dictate our beliefs. Hart is emphatic on this point: "That a man

---

[1] Bernard Hart, "The Psychology of Insanity," p. 61 and p. 62 n.

generally knows why he thinks in a certain way, and why he does certain things, is a widespread and cherished belief of the human race. It is for the most part an erroneous one"[1]

Hart illustrates from cases of insanity. It may seem strange that a man should believe himself to be a millionaire or a royal personage, when clearly his circumstances are incompatible with what he believes. The explanation, says Hart, is that the man is victim of a morbid sentiment of such emotional force, that it repels all evidence which runs contrary to it; the evidence is either not perceived or is explained away. And what is true of the insane is true in less degree of the sane. We all tend to neglect evidence which is in conflict with a sentiment of strong emotional tone, and to accept easily evidence which harmonizes with it. The best of scientists has to make an effort to be alert to evidence which may invalidate the conclusions of a lifetime; he has to make an effort to give full value to the arguments of a rival scientist of whom he is jealous. The selection exercised by a mind dominated by a sentiment can be seen where religion or patriotism is in question. The facts of the universe, the language of the Bible, are the same for Protestant, Roman Catholic, and Agnostic; but they are very differently interpreted. The rights and wrongs of the Great War seemed very different to Englishmen, Frenchmen, Germans, Americans, and to neutral observers. The confirmed party politician is incapable of seeing any good in the arguments and proposals of the leaders of the opposing party.

The process by which we supply ourselves with plausible reasons for believing what we want to believe and for doing what we want to do, and for not believing what we should dislike believing, and for not doing what we should dislike doing, is called *rationalization*; and it is a great advance in self-knowledge and in knowledge of others when we become aware of this bias and can allow for it. Rationalization plays a big part both in personal conduct and in the life of groups and societies.

---

[1] Hart, *op. cit.*, p. 65.

The process of keeping in separate compartments of the same mind ideas which are incompatible with one another is termed *dissociation*. In few of us is there a complete harmony of all our thoughts and feelings. We want incompatibles; and if there are in us incompatible sentiments with strong emotional tone, they may be able to resist disruption and to remain together in the same mind. Another method of dealing with troublesome ideas and troublesome feelings is to repress them, to refuse them expression and as far as possible to thrust them out of consciousness. They do not necessarily cease to exist in the mind which represses them, and repressed emotions can work powerfully and often harmfully. Modern psycho-therapeutic literature is full of illustrations of this.

By a careful choice of linking ideas some part of the energy attaching to one sentiment may be diverted to reinforce the energy attaching to another sentiment. Such siphoning of emotion is part of the technique of propaganda. Thus the cause of a political party may be much helped if it is associated in the minds of voters with the national cause; the candidate prints the Union Jack on his election literature in the hope that some of the powerful emotions called up by that symbol may become attached to his candidature. Similarly, much of the economic propaganda of the last twenty-five years has been supported by arguments which were not really economic, but were only thinly disguised vehicles for conveying nationalistic prejudices.

Many phenomena of human life, both that of individuals and of societies, can only be understood in terms of sentiments, a thesis which will find abundant illustration in the remaining chapters of this book.

While the more important sentiments are of considerable tenacity and duration, they are subject to modification and they may disappear entirely. Thus, a man may experience a series of romantic attachments to different women; in each case there is the growth and decay of a sentiment. Our friendships, which are sentiments, may decay. A man's attachment to a political party or to a religious denomination may cease. What we know as conversion is the rearrangement of the constituents of an old sentiment in a new sentiment or sentiments. Sentiments, though they are resistant, do change by the impact of new facts and of new experiences; and they are most altered, in spite of their resistance, by human reflection and by human reason. For when the maximum has been said about human irrationality, it remains true that the most important fact about man is that he does reason.

FURTHER READING

ed. F. C. Bartlett	The Study of Society.
C. A. Ellwood	Introduction to Social Psychology.
M. Ginsberg	The Psychology of Society.
B. Hart	The Psychology of Insanity.
J. Huxley	The Uniqueness of Man.
A. F. Shand	The Foundations of Character.
P. Sorokin	Contemporary Sociological Theories, Chapter XI.
R. S. Woodworth	Psychology, 1940 edition.

CHAPTER IV

PATTERNS OF BEHAVIOUR

FROM a variety of causes there is a strong tendency to repetition in the behaviour of individuals, and to similarities in behaviour amongst persons of the same society. In the first place, there is the likelihood that individuals of the same or similar natures confronted with the same or similar situations will react to them in the same or similar manners. In the second place, nervous systems adjust themselves to repetitions of behaviour in such a way that with each repetition that form of response becomes easier, until in many cases it becomes automatic. In the third place, there is a whole group of processes which are commonly classed together as imitation;[1] they include such very different processes as the sympathetic induction of emotion from one individual to another, the easy acceptance of ideas from individuals or groups whose prestige is high, and the rational imitation of the behaviour of others. Furthermore, fear of the unknown tends to produce conformity, the familiar pattern of behaviour has been tested and is known to work not too badly, whereas innovation may have unpredictable consequences. Lastly, when once a manner of doing things has become established, there usually grows round it a sentiment of a pleasant nature, so that acting in accordance with that pattern is in itself pleasurable.

In short, we tend to repeat our own past behaviour, and we tend to behave as our neighbours do. It is usually easier to do again something which has been done before rather than to do something new; it is easier to do something which others have done or are doing rather than to do something different. We follow precedents more easily than we devise

---

[1] On imitation see McDougall's " Introduction to Social Psychology," p. 102 *et seq.*, or Ellwood's " Introduction to Social Psychology," p. 224 *et seq.*

new forms, and in this manner we economize thought and emotion and effort. Human life would be intolerable, and indeed impossible, at any high level, if we had to think out for ourselves and repeatedly, the best way of doing a thousand things which we have to do. Fortunately it is not necessary ; a large part of the business of life becomes a matter of habit. Dressing and undressing, using a typewriter, finding our way about the streets of a town, are familiar examples of activities which we perform at first slowly and laboriously, but which later on we do without effort and with little conscious attention. And also we are helped in many situations by observing how other people do things, so that we need not try out for ourselves ways of doing them. In the sphere of morality we should be hard put to it if we had to think out repeatedly the issues involved in our responses to the situations of life. For the most part our behaviour follows patterns which have become well established in our natures, and to a large extent these patterns of behaviour are those prevalent in the society of which we are members.

A little reflection will make us realize the pervasiveness and the importance of social patterns of behaviour. There is scarcely any sphere of life to which they do not extend. They include a vast number of techniques of all kinds ; they include all sorts of social and moral codes ; they include groupings and relationships of many kinds. They shape the life of each one of us to a large extent ; and to a large extent the differences between societies are due to differences in their social patterns. It is possible to classify these social patterns in many ways ; for our purposes we shall concern ourselves with two important aspects of them : (*a*) the extent to which their existence and their significance are consciously realized ; (*b*) the extent to which there is social pressure to conform to them.

With regard to the first point, many patterns of behaviour prevail over so great an area that alternatives are not witnessed, and they are of such antiquity that no memory survives of alternative ways of doing things. In such a case a pattern of behaviour is followed as a matter of course with little or no consciousness that anything else could be done. (This does not exclude awareness of the process and interest in its variations within the pattern.) This we may call *mere custom*, the continuous doing of a certain thing in a certain way by members of a society in whose minds there is no consciousness of alternative ways existent or possible. How food is cooked, how clothes are washed, how houses are built, how ricks are thatched, are familiar examples of mere custom in operation. Similarly there are bridal customs and burial customs, local festivals and local superstitions, ways of doing things and ways of thought which are accepted unreflectingly. Such customs can be of enormous tenacity: men and women go on doing things in a certain way just because they have been done so in the past, and they do not inquire whether there is any longer a good reason for doing so, if ever there was one. There are customs still followed in English villages, such as the lighting of bonfires on New Year's Eve, which had their origins thousands of years back in pagan rites.

But though customs are tenacious of existence, they do change or disappear. In the first place, alterations in the size and density of populations may weaken and ultimately destroy them. When a village has grown into a town, it is no longer possible to greet each passer-by. Upton Sinclair describes in one of his novels the wedding feast which a Hungarian immigrant to Chicago makes on the occasion of his daughter's marriage, and the difficulties into which he gets because he tries to practise the open hospitality traditional in the Carpathian village from which he had come. A second solvent of custom is the introduction of new techniques, which may cause innovations far beyond their immediate sphere of operation; thus railway travel has done much to modify or to destroy the observance of caste rules in India. A third great solvent of custom is contact of cultures. The traveller learns that the ways of doing things with which he is familiar are not the only ways. And he teaches as well as learns. And all improvements in means of communication tend to operate in the same way. Once men know that there are alternative ways of doing things, some of them at least will begin to think about their rationale. The foundation has been laid for an analytical habit of thought. Some men will canvass possible alternatives to any and every mode of behaviour. When such men express themselves in literature, they frequently employ the device of imagining a man taken from our civilization to a totally different civilization. To this class of writings belong the Utopias. Alternatively, a visitor may be conceived as coming from some alien world to question the customs which most of us take for granted. Voltaire's "L'Ingénu," Lowes Dickinson's "Letters from John Chinaman," and Mr. Wells' "Wonderful Visit" are good examples in this kind.

At the other extreme from *mere custom* there is the deliberate initiation and sustentation of patterns of behaviour. Such, for instance, are the institution of rites, the promulgation of laws, the setting up of organizations for various purposes. Of these there is probably more to-day than at any previous period in history, but they have taken place in all ages. What to-day are mere customs must once have been new and deliberate actions; and much that we now practise consciously and deliberately, with full choice as against possible alternatives, may become mere custom in course of time. And between unconsciousness and full consciousness there are many gradations.

With regard to conformity there is every shade of possibility between no obligation and full obligation. *Mere custom* needs no enforcement; it occurs to no one to depart from it. But there is also a good deal of behaviour, which, whilst it may have some customary character, is not so universal that other ways of doing things may not be conceived or attempted. In such cases modes of behaviour are likely to receive critical attention. They will be reflected upon and discussed; they will be recognized as licit or illicit; if licit, they will be regarded as matters of indifference or as commendable; finally, those modes of behaviour may be insisted upon or they may be prohibited. And the social pressure to conform may take many forms, and may be of varying strengths.

In the first place, the fact that the great majority of persons in a society behave in a certain way gives that mode of behaviour a high prestige, and there is a tendency to regard the nonconformist, who sets his judgment against that of his fellows, as a presumptuous person. Further, it is felt in many societies, especially primitive societies, that innovations may endanger the well-being of others, as well as that of the innovator himself. The nonconformist is therefore regarded with disfavour which may easily become downright disapproval. In that case a rule of behaviour may easily be established. " Social habits," writes Westermarck, " have a strong tendency to become true customs, that is, rules of conduct in addition to their being habits."[1] Not all writers would accept Westermarck's terminology, but I propose using *true custom* of patterns of behaviour, current in a society, to which there has become attached a social pressure to conform. *True custom* is thus distinguished from *mere custom*, in the case of which no pressure to conform is necessary. The observance of a true custom is secured partly by personal habit and partly by public opinion. Coercions may be added, such as those of church discipline, or of legal penalties, or of economic pressure. But even when law supervenes on custom, the element of personal habit usually remains and is an important factor in securing general observance. And when, as happens often in modern societies, new modes of behaviour are prescribed by law, those subject to the law become habituated to them. Custom often develops into law; but also law engenders custom.

But there also exist in most societies spheres of behaviour in which a considerable latitude obtains; there are social patterns which may be generally followed, but failure to conform to which arouses little criticism. Doubtless there are more of such in modern societies than in earlier societies, but they exist even in primitive societies.[2] Such modes of behaviour we may call *social usages*. Thus there are a good many social usages with regard to food, and an individual may be regarded as eccentric if he does not conform to them,

---

[1] Westermarck, " Short History of Marriage," p. 28.
[2] W. G. Sumner, " Folkways," p. 54.

but there is no strong compulsion upon him to do so. And so it is with regard to clothing, and with regard to many other matters. But eating, or not eating, certain foods, and the manner of doing so, may come to have religious or political significance; in such a case the usage has been institutionalized, and conformity is demanded. Similarly with regard to clothing, it is one thing to dress conventionally or unconventionally, and quite another thing to wear or not to wear a uniform; in the latter case a particular mode of dress has been institutionalized.

* * * *

We are now ready to consider the nature of a social institution. The term has been much overworked, and a surprising variety of definitions will be found in sociological literature. The definition which I propose is as follows:

A social institution is a relationship approved by society, or by a section of society, together with the approved ideas and approved behaviour relevant to that relationship.

It may be well to consider more closely what is meant by, and what is involved in, a social relationship. By social relationship is meant that certain present circumstances or certain past actions render appropriate certain forms of behaviour between the persons concerned. Thus men and women have sexual intercourse and children are born, or may be born; it has been widely felt from a very early period that mating, issuing in parenthood, makes appropriate certain types of subsequent (and, for that matter, precedent) behaviour, including, as a rule, common residence and the sharing of economic burdens. We describe this by saying that the human race has instituted marriage and the family; it recognizes the relationships of husband and wife, of parent and child, of brother and sister, and it expects certain modes of behaviour between them. Or again, in past times a victor spared the life of a vanquished foe, and society recognized his right to control the captive's actions and to appropriate the results of his labours. Society instituted slavery; it recognized the relationship of master and slave, and it allowed certain modes of behaviour. Usually the application to any person of the term describing a relationship tells us something of the probable past history and of the probable behaviour of that person and of the other parties to the relationship. The social recognition and the social approval of a relationship constitute it an institution; and they imply the recognition and approval of a body of ideas and of modes of behaviour.

Among the major social institutions of mankind are: marriage and the family, property, war, slavery, state, and church.[1] Other examples of important social institutions are: primogeniture, kingship, priesthood. In every case there is the threefold aspect of relationship, sustaining ideas and feelings, behaviour. Many of the major institutions have attached to them subordinate institutions, are indeed complexes of institutions. Such an institution as our British House of Lords makes use of a number of other institutions such as primogeniture and episcopate and representation.

W. J. Sumner drew a useful distinction between what he called "crescive" institutions and "enacted" institutions. The former are such as grow up gradually, so that it is often difficult to say at what stage they became institutions. The latter are such as have been deliberately created at some well-defined period. As an example of a crescive institution we may cite marriage and the family, whose rudimentary forms are to be found in sub-human species. As an example of enacted institution we may take the County Councils of this country which were deliberately created by the Local Government Act of 1888.

In the case of old and widespread social institutions of crescive type the origin may be so remote and so hard to discern that the institutional nature of the relationship and the behaviour may not be perceived. Thus Aristotle thought of

---

[1] It should be noted that the same term is often used of a social institution, a social group, and sometimes also of the material objects in which the social institution and the social group manifest themselves. Thus family, church, college, all of them denote (a) a social institution; (b) a social group; whilst in the case of the last two the word denotes also (c) a building. In the case of property the term denotes both the social institution and the things, material or immaterial, in respect of which the approved pattern of behaviour obtains.

slavery as being an inevitable product of the differences in human abilities. But anthropological research has indicated that slavery only appears at a certain stage of social development; and in the last hundred years or so it has disappeared from the greater part of the world. So also with regard to war, which some have regarded as a universal phenomenon of human society, it is well established that a number of primitive peoples are without the institution, and find great difficulty in conceiving of it. Marriage and the family come nearer to being universal and necessary features of human life, but even with regard to them there is a wide gap between such rudimentary forms as are to be found among the anthropoid apes, or among some primitive peoples, and the well-marked and socially regulated forms of relationships generally to be found.

An established social institution of any importance will be marked by having a code of behaviour attached to it, which is well understood by members of the group among whom the institution obtains; and the observance of the code will be safeguarded by social pressure of the group upon its members. Often the law will compel observance of the code. Often those who break it are regarded as transgressors against the injunctions of religion, and in many societies they have been liable to ecclesiastical rebuke and penalties. Sometimes the penalty is expulsion from a society; sometimes it is ostracism within the society. Always there will be the weight of public opinion pressing upon the recalcitrant. But also, with the passing of time, sentiments grow round institutions, so that their maintenance is a matter of pride and pleasure. And to a considerable extent institutional behaviour tends to become customary behaviour, so that men conform to it without reflection. An institution which has survived several human generations is not easily destroyed; it is usually taken for granted by those who have grown up within its influence, and it is to them a part of their social environment, moulding their thought and behaviour to an extent of which they are usually impercipient. And the mere fact that an institution holds the field renders difficult, if not impossible, alternative modes of behaviour.

Professor Ginsberg, in his "Psychology of Society," writes that social institutions are "definite and sanctioned forms or modes of relationships between social beings in respect to one another, or to some external object."[1] The reference to the external object is a useful one. Feudalism was a relationship of men to men associated with a relationship of men to land. The social institution of property allows men to stand in a peculiar relation to things, that of exclusive control; but the relationship to things would have little meaning if there were not involved a relationship with other men, an understanding that they have no right of control. A particular category of this double relationship of men to things and of men to men is the use of symbols. We sometimes speak of a national flag as an institution, but the institution is really the sanctioned understanding that the flag shall mean something to members of the nation. The same applies to all symbols; what is truly institutionalized is the agreement that the thing shall have a certain meaning. We agree that certain sounds shall convey certain ideas, that certain marks shall stand for certain sounds; language and notation have been agreed upon and, whilst we may elliptically speak of the things as institutions, the true institution is the agreed interpretation and use of them. If we understand this, we may accept the study of symbols as part of the study of institutions.

The external object of Professor Ginsberg's definition may be a period of time; one species of social institution is the observance of certain days or seasons, such as Lent or St. George's Day. Many observances of set times are not to be ranked higher than social usages; they are recognized, and there is some expectation that they will be followed, but there is no strong sanction behind them and no sense of outraged relationship if they are neglected. But others are truly institutional; their observance is part of the behaviour demanded of those who stand in a certain relationship. Thus the man or woman who neglected Sunday observance in Victorian England was showing contempt for that which was

---

[1] The Psychology of Society, p. 122.

one of the marks of a relationship, that existing between men and women of the same religion, a religion which had the powerful endorsement of society, so that to flout its observances was to flout society. Sunday observance was truly and highly institutional then; to-day it is little more than social usage. In the political sphere, May Day is a recognized festival of the Labour parties everywhere, and to neglect its observance would not improve the chances of any aspirant to leadership; May Day must be reckoned as a political institution.

Many institutions have subsidiary institutions attached to them; they are indeed complexes or constellations of institutions. As an illustration one may cite the modern State with its multitude of associated institutions: representative government, secret ballot, permanent Civil Service, political symbolism. Similarly Churches and Universities have subordinate institutions: priesthood, fasts and festivals, sacraments, are examples of those attaching to Church; senates, professorships, conferment of degrees, are examples of those attaching to Universities.

System is a word which is employed very freely, but which is seldom defined; we speak of the feudal system, of the capitalist system, of the party system, and so on. A system, when the term is applied to human relationships, is a species of social institution; it is a recognized distribution of rôles and functions for purposes wholly or partly held in common. Thus under the feudal system each grade in society had its recognized rights and duties, and the common purpose was the maintenance of order and the supplying of economic needs. Under capitalism there is another allocation of rôles in the economic sphere. In politics the party system secures concerted action of those who think roughly alike on public questions and establishes conventions of conduct between opposing groups: it provides a division of function between a legislative and administrative group and a group checking and modifying their actions by criticism; it provides, moreover, for a periodic exchange of functions between the groups. The common purpose is the carrying on of government with some decision by allowing majority rule, and at the same time securing a form of government more or less responsive to the different elements in public opinion and the changes in it.

* * *

Whilst some social patterns are to be found over the greater part of human society and over most of time, there are many others which are confined to a particular locality, to a particular society, or to a particular period of time. Every society and every group has its peculiar patterns of behaviour; and the differences between societies and between groups are in large measure due to differences in the prevalent patterns, and especially to differences in their social institutions. The study of social institutions, of their genesis and range and interconnections and modifications, is the most important part of the study of society.

In conclusion, a short account will be given of four of them which are notable because they have been widespread and because their influence upon human affairs has been so great. They are marriage and family, property, war, and slavery.

Marriage and family are found universally among men, though often in forms which seem very strange to us of Western civilization. They are a social institution (or, if the reader prefers it, a pair of closely linked social institutions) which clearly originated out of the long immaturity of the human young, and whose essence is an association of some duration for the procreation and rearing of children. Westermarck defines marriage as "a relation of one or more men to one or more women which is recognized by custom or law, and involves certain rights and duties both in the case of the parties entering the union, and in the case of the children born of it." Almost always marriage and family are understood to involve economic co-operation and social companionship. The association of several men with several women (group marriage) is very rare. Association of one individual of one sex with several individuals of the other sex (polygamy) is found in many societies; of the two forms of polygamy the association of one man with several women (polygyny) is much more frequently found than the association of one woman with several men (polyandry). But even in societies which permit polygamy the proportion of polygamous marriages is usually small, since wide discrepancies in the number of the sexes are not common. The association of one man with one woman (monogamy) is found as sole pattern in many societies at all stages of development, and it is the only sanctioned form in contemporary Western civilization, lifelong pair marriage being the norm. But just as societies sanction marriage and thereby make it a social institution, so also most societies sanction, on varying conditions, divorce, the termination of a marriage.

The relationship of marriage is recognized and regulated by law, which enumerates categories of persons between whom it may not be contracted. The law insists on permanence of the relationship, subject to dissolution which it will allow and proclaim in certain contingencies. The law also recognizes its exclusiveness; thus, in this and the other countries of Christendom, polygamy is forbidden. It further recognizes, and will enforce, economic responsibilities of the spouses to one another and to their offspring. Marriage is also a matter of concern to the Churches, which have their own rules with regard to it, rules which do not always coincide with those of the State; and over and above their rules, and such discipline as they may be able to enforce, the whole influence of the Churches is directed to maintaining the permanence and the exclusiveness of the marriage tie. And in addition to the pressure of State and of Church there is the diffused pressure of public opinion; those who flout the institution of marriage are regarded with social disapproval which may amount to social ostracism.

Attached to the social institution of marriage there is a cluster of usages, more or less recognized, more or less expected; they rest upon assumptions which are scarcely the less binding because they are often tacit. "Will you marry me?" says Jack to Jill, and the words have an enormous unexpressed, but understood content. In England, between persons of the middle class, at the present time, the words mean something like this:

"Will you, on some day within the next year or two, leave your parents' home and meet me at either church or registry office, so that there, before properly appointed officials and in set form, we may publicly declare our intention to spend the rest of our lives together ? Will you, after a short holiday with me, come to a house where you and I can live together ? Will you be mate to me and to no other man, on the understanding that I be mate to you and to no other woman ? Will you agree that I shall work to obtain the income necessary to maintain us and the children who may be born to us, whilst you undertake responsibility for the domestic arrangements ? " . . .

And so on. It is much to be compressed into four words, but this and a great deal more is conveyed, because marriage is one of our major social institutions, a great pattern of behaviour with many subordinate patterns of behaviour, and the implications of marriage are well understood. The implications differ in detail from age to age, from country to country, in the different social classes, and almost between each pair. Marriage was one thing in Victorian England ; it is another thing in the England of to-day. It is a different thing again in countries where polygamy is allowed. And marriage has taken many strange and scarcely recognizable forms. Yet all of these are forms of one social institution, the essence of which is that the sex relationship is made part of a wider, durable relationship, and that society recognizes this relationship and the responsibilities created by it.

Property is another of the social institutions of mankind which is to be found everywhere and always in some form. "Property in its most general sense," writes Beaglehole, " may be taken to mean the exclusive use, enjoyment and control of those things which are of value in so far as, directly or indirectly, they serve to satisfy the fundamental needs of the organism."[1] Property rights are defined and enforced by law in every country where there is a developed machinery

---

[1] E. Beaglehole, "Property," p. 15.

of government; and more primitive societies have their own methods of regulation. Commonly the sanctions of religion are placed behind property rights; " Thou shalt not steal " and " Cursed be he that removeth his neighbour's landmark " have their counterparts in other codes. And public opinion usually supports the owner of property in his claim. But, again, whilst the social institution of property is to be found in some form everywhere, the actual forms vary very much from society to society. In an Eskimo tribe personal possessions are very limited in range, whilst the whole tribe is conceived to have rights over hunting grounds and the more important instruments by which livelihood is obtained. In nineteenth-century England, on the contrary, most property was the property of individuals, and claims were advanced to almost unrestricted control by individuals of vast tracts of land and of mines and factories. Property rights may change rapidly, and in our time and land there have been important modifications of the laws of inheritance and there has been increasing control by the State over the uses to which land and plant may be put.

Property rights are socially important as incentives to the production and conservation of wealth. They are also socially important in that they help to lay the foundations of class differentiation, and in that they may become the basis of domination and of exploitation. This is especially so when individuals or small groups own large tracts of land, or own such large-scale means of production as a modern factory; they are then placed in a position of great bargaining advantage as against those who have no such property. This process has gone far in modern times, and at the same time much ownership of land which was formerly an ill-defined trusteeship has become ownership without recognized responsibilities. Property in such circumstances becomes a means of levying a toll on the fruit of other men's labours rather than a guarantee that those who labour shall enjoy the fruits of their toil. It was a contemplation of the first form of ownership, the ownership by a peasant of the small piece of land which he and his family cultivated, which led Arthur Young to write : " Property is the magic which turns sand into gold." It was contemplation of the latter kind of ownership which led Proudhon to write: "La propriété, c'est le vol." In both aphorisms there is a measure of truth.

Subsidiary to the social institution of property are the social institutions of inheritance and of bequest. The former is restricted to the family and it is closely regulated in the majority of societies; sometimes it takes the form of primogeniture, less often of ultimogeniture, to serve the double purpose of securing an undisputed succession and of keeping the property intact. But in such cases, more particularly in the case of primogeniture, the heir is usually in substance trustee for the family, though in form he may be the owner. The right of bequest is of late development, mainly of importance in individualistic societies.

War is a social institution which is found almost everywhere, but not quite everywhere; there are scattered about the world a few tribes at a low level of livelihood and of social development among whom it is unknown; for the most part these are still at the stage of food gathering, not having attained to either domestication of animals nor to cultivation of crops. But war would appear to be an almost universal feature of societies in which there is any considerable development of property and of social organization. And once warfare is established, it tends to greater accumulation of property by some individuals and some groups, and to more highly developed and hierarchical organization of societies. War has been defined as "armed conflict between population groups conceived as organic entities."[1] Wars have been fought for many reasons: to settle disputes about boundaries or kindred matters, for the sake of plunder, for prestige and aggrandisement, to impose a culture, to assist an ally. And to some men war becomes an end in itself, a joyous sport.

Wars have ranged from those of a mild nature, much noise and fury to a small number of casualties, to wars of great ferocity and destructiveness. Much of the warfare between

---

[1] Encyclopædia of Religion and Ethics, s.v. War.

primitive peoples is of the former type. Some of the most savage wars have been inspired or supported by religious fanaticism. Nearly always there is to be found some regulation of warfare: there have been generally accepted conventions as to the sacredness of heralds, the methods of declaring war, the non-use of certain weapons, the treatment of non-combatants and of prisoners, the etiquette of armistices, and many other matters. With the development of civilization much of this has been embodied in codes of international law, accepted in principle by the leading states, but dependent for its observance on their good faith only. In many societies, both primitive and more advanced, a high degree of chivalry has sometimes been displayed, a force in a stronger position voluntarily equalizing the conditions of combat. But by its nature war engenders brutality, and its urgencies break down scruples; it is not surprising, therefore, that the rules established are often violated, and that their violation is even more often alleged.

The social institution of slavery, though widespread and of great antiquity, is not universal and does not appear to be primitive. Few of the societies which are still in the stage of mere food gathering have got it, and those which have it are surmised to have learned it from neighbours in a further stage of social development. It is more common among the pastoral peoples, and it is found more often than not among peoples who practise a fairly simple agriculture. It is supposed to have originated out of war, the prisoner being retained to work instead of being killed; and once the social institution had been established, other ways of making slaves were discovered; the children of slave mothers are usually slaves, and persons may become slaves because of debts, contracted by themselves or by their parents. In classical times exposed infants were sometimes appropriated and reared as slaves. And with a growing market, slave raiding became a common practice. There are also to be found in many societies slaves, dedicated to the service of gods.

The essence of slavery is that one person has the right to control all the actions of another person and to appropriate the fruits of his labours. Many gradations of slavery are to be found, and it is not always easy to delimit the boundary between slavery and freedom. Various limitations may be put upon the power of the master, sometimes by custom, sometimes by law, sometimes by religion. Thus there has often been some protection against extremes of violence, though that protection has usually been slight. And often there has been some possibility of the slave earning some small amount for himself, whether by sheer grace of his master, or with a stronger social sanction. The chances of attaining to freedom have varied much. There has been great variation, too, in the extent to which the slave has been permitted to form stable family relationships: in some societies, both ancient and modern, a slave has been held incapable of contracting a true marriage. There has been great variation, too, in the extent of culture to which a slave might attain; commonly the life of the slave has been rough and ignorant, but in the Roman empire a large part of the intelligentsia were slaves. On the other hand it was forbidden, in some of the American states, in the nineteenth century to teach slaves to read or to write, and they were forbidden to be teachers or preachers. Social status amongst slaves has depended partly upon occupation, household slaves ranking above field slaves, and field slaves above industrial slaves. In part, also, it has followed the status of the master. Slaves of a different race, or born in a different society, have usually ranked beneath native slaves of the same race. Attitudes towards sacred slaves have often been curiously ambivalent; they have been regarded with peculiar respect and with great contempt.

Modern ethical views, and in part modern economic developments, have caused the social institution of slavery to decay, but there are still in the world several millions of slaves, almost entirely in Asia and Africa.

FURTHER READING

L. B. Ballard	Social Institutions.
M. Ginsberg	The Psychology of Society.
L. T. Hobhouse	Social Development.
W. James	Principles of Psychology.
R. M. Maciver	Elements of Social Science.
Osborn and Neumeyer	The Community and Society.
W. G. Sumner	Folkways.
Sumner and Keller	The Science of Society.

CHAPTER V

THE RÔLE OF IDEAS IN SOCIETY

UNDERLYING social behaviour, that is to say, behaviour which is characteristic of a group of persons, there is social thought, that is to say, thinking (and feeling) which is common to members of the group. Some small part of this thinking may be merely the similar thinking of similar individuals in similar circumstances; but usually there has been mental interaction, so that the thought itself is a social product. Whilst it is often impossible to separate thought from behaviour, it can be distinguished from it; and ordinary language, as well as the more specialized language of social scientists, does sometimes so distinguish it. In this chapter we deal with some of the recognized forms of social thought, discuss how such thought originates and operates, and try to show its place in the total structure of society.

Durkheim has called attention to the manner in which the thoughts and feelings which result from mental interaction, though they originate in the thinking and feeling of individual minds and must operate through individual minds to produce effects in behaviour, are yet to the individual in part environmental, imposing themselves upon him from without.[1] These collective thoughts, which are everyone's thoughts and no one's thoughts, are shaping forces, determining to a large extent the nature of a society and much of the behaviour of

---

[1] "Voilà donc des manières d'agir, de penser et de sentir qui présentent cette remarquable propriété qu'elles existent en dehors des consciences individuelles. Non seulement ces types de conduite ou de pensée sont extérieurs à l'individu, mais ils sont doués d'une puissance impérative et coercitive en vertu de laquelle ils s'imposent à lui, qu'il le veuille ou non." E. Durkheim, "Les Règles de la Méthode Sociologique," p. 6.

each of its members. Of this body of collective thought[1] part is relatively fluid and unformulated, but part is "precipitated"[2] into formulæ of various kinds: creeds, codes, dogmas, doctrines, principles, and (juridical) laws.

The mental aspects of patterns of behaviour, such as were discussed in the last chapter, are described collectively as the *mores* of a society. They are common judgments underlying prevalent modes of behaviour: recognition that these are the ways in which things are done, together usually with a presumption that things are best done in these ways. Where the presumption is imperative we have to do with conventions or with morals, usually with social sanctions of some kind attached to them to secure conformity. The difference between conventions and morals is that in the former case the obligation is conceived as being social but not ethical; those who do not conform are regarded as being clumsy or ignorant or misguided, but not selfish or wicked; whereas morals are ethical standards of behaviour, and to fall short of them is regarded as selfishness or wickedness. A law may formulate and enforce a convention of society, or it may enforce conformity to some part of the moral code. Thus arson, burglary, forgery, are considered to be not only criminal, but also evidences of turpitude; whilst, on the other hand, there are many actions punishable by law, such as exceeding the permissible time for parking a car, which are recognized to be merely technical offences. *Mores* of a negative character are often called taboos, and they may be ethical, or they may be merely conventional in nature. The whole body of *mores*, though it may include some mutually discrepant elements, tends to have a consistency, which gives a general character to a society. This

---

[1] The writer wishes to make clear that while he considers it legitimate and serviceable to speak of the history of ideas, of the development of ideas, and of collective thought, he realizes that thinking can only be done in the minds of individual men, and that ideas develop by the thinking of individual men stimulated by contact with other individual men. But whilst thinking can only take place in brains (so far as we know), that which has been thought can be stored either in brains or in certain material symbols, notably in books. An idea may exist in a manuscript or in a printed book during a period of time when it has no existence in the brain of any living man, and it may ultimately be appropriated and used by men of a later period. A good example of this is Mendel's theory of heredity, which was neglected for several decades and was re-discovered after his death in the obscure magazine in which he had published it.

[2] The phrase is Durkheim's; *op. cit.*, p. 12.

general character of a society is called its *ethos*. Ethos is a holistic conception, and the ethos of a society may be compared with the character of an individual.

In the case of the *mores* the ideas are related to definite modes of conduct. There are, however, many cases of ideas which are powerfully operative in society, and which may receive a measure of recognition and approval, without corresponding with any specific form of behaviour, though undoubtedly influencing behaviour. Such are many creeds and dogmas, whether they be religious, political, or scientific. Such are ideals, which are conceptions of what might be, or of what ought to be. Such, too, are many dominant ideas, less clearly formulated, as, for instance, the nineteenth-century belief in the fact and inevitability of progress; or the even less defined, but potent, complex of ideas which Matthew Arnold denounced as Philistinism. And we should remember that there is in every age, and in every society, a body of assumptions, constraining that society, which are so unchallenged that they lie for the most part below the threshold of consciousness.

The structure of a society is sustained, and the behaviour of its members is in a large measure determined, by a body of ideas; and if those ideas should change, that structure and that behaviour will change, though probably with a time-lag, which may be a long one. The history of ideas is, therefore, an important part of the history of mankind. It is impossible to measure the effects on social structure and on social behaviour of the idea of one God, creator of the universe and father of all men, but these effects have certainly been very great. Great, too, have been the effects of ideas of fate, contained in various forms in a number of religions and philosophies. The modern world could not have come into existence if there had not emerged and spread the idea of a reign of law throughout nature. Among political ideas which have been important in the history of mankind are the doctrine of natural rights, the doctrine of *laissez faire*, and the body of Marxist doctrines which in our day has brought about, or more strictly has helped to bring about, the Russian Revolution, and has taken form in the Soviet régime. The reader can think of many other ideas which have been powerful in human affairs. To such ideas we may conveniently apply the term Idea-Force, which the French sociologist Alfred Fouillée introduced,[1] though he used it with a somewhat different connotation.

But men do not think *in vacuo*; they think in concrete social situations, and their thinking is conditioned by those social situations, which include their geographical environment, their technological level, their economic relationships, their social status, the social institutions of their society, the systems of thought and feeling prevalent in that society, and its political relations with other societies. A change in any of these may induce changes in ideas, again usually with a time-lag. Thus the invention of the telescope led to a new knowledge of the universe, and this new knowledge disturbed profoundly theological conceptions. The coming of power machinery and of large-scale production contributed to a change in men's thinking about property rights, about the responsibilities of a society to its members in misfortune, and about many other matters. In our own day the invention of the aeroplane has obviously influenced British thinking about international politics.

Reference was made in an earlier chapter to the part played by wishes in colouring thought; there can be no doubt that collective thoughts are often rationalizations, or include elements of that nature. The ideas prevalent at any given time in a society, or in a group within a society, will depend in part upon the major interests of the members of the society or group. Among these interests economic interests are likely to play an important part, but there will be many other interests, such as that of the prestige of the group. In modern times those who perceive, or think they perceive, that the social philosophy of a group to which they do not belong is coloured by its situation and by its interests often indicate their perception, real or supposed, of the distortion by calling

---

[1] Alfred Fouillée, "Morale des Idées-Forces."

the social philosophy an "ideology." There is a small but increasing number of persons who attempt the difficult task of examining their own social philosophy in order to discover its ideological elements.

The prevailing social institutions of a society limit for most men the range of their thinking. It was almost impossible for men living in a feudal society to think in other than feudal terms; they could not imagine free contract or a high degree of mobility. To members of such a society as ours, which allows liberal rights of bequest, it seems to most men to be a matter of course that they should control ownership after their own lifetime; but over a large part of the world, and over a large part of time, it has seemed otherwise. It is difficult in a society in which war is a recognized social institution to conceive of a warless world; but to some of the Eskimos, brought up in societies in which there is no such social institution, stories of warfare seem so strange as to be almost incredible. Men are accustomed to certain social institutions from early childhood, and these hold the field; few have the inclination or the ability to examine their history or their justification, and the general pre-supposition is that what exists is right. Thinking is therefore likely to be thinking within the limits imposed by the acceptance of existing social institutions.

Furthermore, the range of thought depends to some extent upon the nature of the social controls and the spirit in which they are exercised. Penalties may be attached to the expression of new ideas, still more to any active propagation of them. And whilst new ideas sometimes make headway against powerful opposition, this is by no means always the case. A moderate amount of persecution may stimulate the spread of a new doctrine, especially if the persecution is intermittent. But a deliberate, ruthless, and continuous persecution is often successful. And, similarly, new ideas may be imposed on groups of men by coercion.[1] But there is no need to go to

---

[1] On this see G. Mosca, "The Ruling Class," pp. 191-92. Mosca cites the failure of Christianity to obtain a foothold in Persia, the forcible conversion of the Saxons to Christianity by Charlemagne, the eradication of Buddhism from India, the rapid spread of Mohammedanism, and gives other illustrations in support of the thesis that doctrines may be imposed or may be suppressed by force.

the length of persecution; much may be done by censorships and by other controls of the dissemination of information and of views, much by propaganda, and perhaps most of all by the indoctrination of the young. If once a generation can be produced whose members think it wrong to speculate outside well-marked boundaries of thought, such an attitude is self perpetuating. As a matter of history there have been few ages and few societies in which wide-ranging speculation has been other than exceptional.

Ideas, therefore, are both causes and effects in society. The interactions between thoughts and situations are so often complex and so often obscure that it is not to be wondered at that the nature of these interactions has given rise to much controversy, to the battle of the idealists and the realists.[1] It is a controversy which may proceed almost interminably and inconclusively. Few sociologists take an extreme idealist position; they are too well aware of the changes in thought which have often followed changes in situation, and they are suspicious of simplicist theories of social development. Most of them accept therefore the view that ideas are conditioned, that is to say that they bear marks of the social situations in which they are conceived and developed. But this leaves open many questions as to the manner and degree of conditioning. Ideas are coloured by social situations, but that is not to say that they merely reflect them, as some realists assert. In the first place, the same social situation may give rise to ideas of different kinds as men react differently to it. And some of these reactions may be very surprising. The

---

[1] The issue between the two schools can be put very sharply by one or two quotations:—

"The world of Fact, artistic or æsthetic, scientific, moral, political, economic, is what the spirit builds round itself, creating it out of its own substance, while itself in creating it grows within." J. A. Smith (quoted Hetherington & Muirhead, "Social Purpose.")

and in contrast:

"All intellectual and moral history, all the political and social history of humanity, is a reflexion of its economic history." M. Bakunin, "Dieu et L'Etat."

whilst Karl Marx states very clearly the opposition between his own realist philosophy and the idealist philosophy of Hegel:

"To Hegel the life process of the human brain, i.e., the process of thinking, which, under the name of "the Idea," he even transforms into an independent subject, is the demiurgos of the real world, and the real world is only the external phenomenal form of "the Idea." With me, on the contrary, "the Idea" is nothing else than the material world reflected by the human mind, and translated into forms of thought." Karl Marx, Introduction to "Das Kapital."

realists are often guilty of *post factum* reasoning; this idea has emerged from such a situation, therefore this idea was bound to emerge from such a situation. But if it had not emerged, they would not have thought that there was any such necessity. It is difficult to account for the universalism of the Jewish prophets of the Exile as a necessary consequence of the national situation at that time; indeed, if universalist ideas had not in point of fact emerged till later, it would probably have been argued that they could not emerge in such circumstances. It might well have been argued that ideas of an opposite kind, a bitter and self-centred nationalist philosophy, must of necessity emerge. And so it did; there is abundance of it in the prophetic writings.[1] But the significant fact is that precisely in this seemingly unfavourable situation an ethic of remarkable generosity and breadth of view did emerge also.[2]

It is furthermore a fact that ideas, once originated and however originated, often develop according to their own internal logic. The idea which arose from a specific social situation is frequently generalized and elaborated, and corollaries are drawn from it which may bear little superficial resemblance to the original propositions. We can point to the elaboration of myths; the original idea, arising perhaps out of some strongly felt need or some unusual and striking happening, is transformed out of all recognition; in its new form it may be applied to modify behaviour. Or in a society of higher intellectual development new principles may be deduced from accepted general principles, as was the case in the history of philosophical radicalism.

It is not difficult to find illustrations to support both the idealist point of view and the realist point of view.[3] Mr. Leonard Woolf argues[4] that the ideas of the *philosophes* brought about the French Revolution, that the ideas which

---

[1] E.g., Joel III, Zechariah XIV.   [2] E.g,. Isaiah II, 1-4, Micah IV, 1-3.
[3] It should be noted that the terms "idealist" and "realist" are used in different senses by political scientists and by philosophers; in this chapter they have been used in the sense of the political scientist.
[4] L. Woolf, "After the Deluge," *passim*; see especially Vol. I, pp. 27 and 106 and Vol. II, p. 143 (Penguin edition).

Marx stigmatized as "bourgeois ideology" preceded the economic system of which Marx thought them to be the product. Max Weber argued that the Protestant ethic had to be developed before capitalism could come into existence. On the other hand Professor E. H. Carr cites[1] a number of instances and opinions to show that ideas follow events: empire precedes imperialism; the doctrine of *laissez faire* was formulated after State regulation had been relaxed, and it was abandoned after State regulation had been resumed. The conclusion which seems warranted is that there is a continuous interaction of ideas and of situations, and that sometimes it is possible to distinguish the former as precedent and sometimes the latter, and often it is impossible to establish any priority.

FURTHER READING

J. B. Bury	History of the Freedom of Thought.
E. H. Carr	The Twenty Years Crisis.
A. V. Dicey	Law and Public Opinion in England.
E. Durkheim	Les Règles de la Méthode Sociologique.
J. A. Hobson	Free Thought in the Social Sciences.
L. T. Hobhouse	Morals in Evolution.
B. Kidd	The Science of Power.
K. Mannheim	Ideology and Utopia.
K. Mannheim	Man and Society.
G. Mosca	The Ruling Class.
R. H. Murray	History of Political Science.
B. Russell	Power.
P. Sorokin	Contemporary Sociological Theories.
M. Weber	The Protestant Ethic and the Spirit of Capitalism.
E. Westermarck	The Origin and Development of the Moral Ideas.
A. N. Whitehead	Adventures of Ideas.

---

[1] E. H. Carr, "The Twenty Years' Crisis," pp. 85-88.

CHAPTER VI

SOCIAL HERITAGE

In an earlier chapter a brief account was given of heredity, the passing on of potentialities from parents to children by physiological process. There is also transmission from generation to generation in another way, that of mental contact. Ideas, sentiments, ways of doing things, can all of them be handed down. Such reception from the past is described as social inheritance, and the total of what has been transmitted is called social heritage.

The lower forms of life have no social heritage; in a large number of cases individuals do not encounter any member of the preceding generation. Social inheritance plays a part, but only a small part, in the life of animals of the higher orders. We have reason to believe that birds learn from their elders: the process of becoming adept at flight is probably shortened; there is evidence that in some cases at least the form of song, though not singing itself, is learned.[1]

It requires little reflection to make us realize that in the case of human beings social inheritance plays a big part. Quite early we are taught cleanly habits. Whilst we should probably in any case utter articulate sounds, the language we actually use is copied from those around us. At a tender age we are instructed in the management of fire. In modern civilized communities we have to be trained carefully to avoid traffic. A little later we have manners instilled into us. Later still we are taught the use of tools, both material tools and also tools of the mind. We acquire, to a large extent unconsciously, customary ways of behaviour; we acquire also attitudes and sentiments and ideas. If it were not for social inheritance we

---

[1] On the subject of tradition amongst animals, consult Fr. Alverdes, " Social Life in the Animal World."

could not live as civilized beings, if indeed we could live at all. And the kind of civilization in which we live is determined in the main by social inheritance.

Let us examine in some detail the elements in social heritage.

In the first place there are *techniques*. A technique has a material aspect and a mental aspect, and techniques may be classed roughly according to the relative importance of the two. In the first category come such techniques as the use of tools and of machinery, agriculture and fishing, writing and printing. In the second category come such techniques as those of mathematics and logical analysis.

In the second place there are *customs, social usages,* and *institutions*. A large part of these in any society at any time have come down from the past; though in each generation modifications may be made both by innovations and by desuetude. The importance of these patterns of behaviour has been stressed in an earlier chapter, and their tenacity has been indicated. There is more plasticity and more actual change in Western civilization to-day than in most previous societies.

In the third place there are *ideas, ideals, sentiments*. We may give as illustrations such ideas as belief in progress, or such an ideal as that of equality, such a sentiment as that of loyalty to one's nation.

Heredity and social heritage do not entirely exhaust that which is transmitted from the past ; there is also the availability of material things which outlast the generation which has created them. Such are buildings, machinery, and furniture ; roads and railways ; harbours, rivers rendered navigable, drainage systems ; tilled land, plantations of trees. These are commonly, but not quite accurately, reckoned as part of social heritage.

The description of the enrichment of the social heritage by successive generations is the task of the historians of culture. All that can be given here is some indication of the nature of the process and of some of the more obvious gains. When we consider that we owe to the past, it is clear that we are in debt to a comparatively small number of great pioneers and to a much larger number of persons who have added, bit by bit, to the sum of human knowledge. The accumulation of small inventions, each carrying a little further some already existent process, has been just as necessary to progress as the first incursions into hitherto unexplored spheres.

The human race is in debt to a number of pioneers who lived before the dawn of written history. We do not know who first taught men to handle fire. Nor do we know the names of the inventors of the earliest tools. The use of fire and the making of the simplest tools date back perhaps half a million years. We do not know who it was who first domesticated animals, or who first planted crops, or who first made pottery, or wove, or used metals; but most of these great advances were probably made within the ten thousand years before the Christian era. Writing and the beginnings of measurement probably date back to 5000 B.C., or thereabouts. Settled life in towns of considerable size probably began in the millennium 4000-3000 B.C.

The period between 800 and 400 B.C. is notable in the history of the human race for its great advances in ethical thought. Here we have names, among which are outstanding those of Lao-Tze, of Gautama Buddha, and of the series of Jewish prophets from Amos to the second Isaiah.

Great advances in knowledge were made in Greece during the fifth and fourth centuries before Christ, especially in mathematics and physics, in medicine, and in what to-day we should call biology. The tools of thought were much improved. Socrates demonstrated a method of close questioning and of following an argument through. Aristotle was the founder of formal logic.

The genius of Rome was practical, and its great contributions during the period from about 100 B.C. to A.D. 400 were in the spheres of engineering and of government and of the formulation of law.

When Europe emerged from the chaos which followed the break-up of the Roman Empire, it received much of its new light from the Arabs, who themselves had drawn upon Greek and Indian sources. Somewhere about A.D. 750 there were the beginnings of chemistry, about A.D. 1000 of algebra, whilst the Hindu numerals reached Europe about A.D. 1200.

The next two centuries saw the introduction to Europe of three material inventions of great importance : printing, the compass, and gunpowder. It was in the thirteenth century also that Roger Bacon laid stress upon experiment rather than upon speculation as a method of advance in knowledge of nature.

The sixteenth and seventeenth centuries produced the telescope and the microscope, enabling us to examine the very distant and the very small. The former of these inventions created a revolution in theological ideas. The latter added enormously to man's mastery over his physical environment.

The seventeenth century witnessed great advances in mathematics, and thus made possible later developments in engineering. The eighteenth century saw the beginnings of modern agriculture, including scientific breeding of stock, and the nineteenth century brought the scientific use of manures.

From the last third of the eighteenth century down to the present time there has been a spate of inventions. The exploitation of natural forces has enabled us to dispense with an enormous amount of mere muscular labour, and has increased human mobility. There were great advances in chemistry, and at a later period in biology, so that to-day we have gone a considerable way in the manipulation, not only of inorganic matter, but also of organic life. And, perhaps of greatest importance for the future of the human race, has been the development of psychology, which is giving to mankind the power to understand itself.

Previous paragraphs have contained a brief and bald account of some of the chief inventions and discoveries which have enriched the social heritage. We think that it is because of this enrichment, and not because of any considerable improvement in our endowment at birth, that in most societies men have attained a higher level of control over things and processes than was the case in the past. A boy in an English secondary school to-day can make calculations which were impossible to Aristotle, not because the boy has better brains than Aristotle had (the odds are heavy that his brains are inferior) but because there are available to him an accumulation of knowledge, a number of instruments and devices, and methods of thinking, which were not available to Aristotle. To illustrate, all the calculations of Aristotle and of his contemporaries had to be made in a clumsy pre-Arabic notation. Our secondary schoolboy will not only be familiar with the Arabic notation, but he will be acquainted with the decimal system, with the use of logarithms, and possibly with the binomial theorem. And these are the mathematical foundations of the miracles of modern engineering, and of much else which was beyond the horizon of Aristotle's thought and competence.

So far we have been writing in this chapter of social heritage and of society, but we need to write of social heritages and of societies. For the content of their social heritage is very different for different groups of men. It is true that there are some elements in it which are the same in all human societies, many more which are found in most human societies; this may be due to independent inventions of similar beings faced with similar needs, or it may be due to diffusion of knowledge, and as to the relative parts played by the two processes there is much controversy. But it is also true that the differences in technical achievement between contemporary societies are, and have been, very striking. The ability to use fire appears to be universal in historic times, but even within the last few centuries there have been found two peoples[1] who did not know how to kindle it. The wheel was unknown in pre-Columban America.[2] The reindeer was domesticated by a large number of tribes in the north of Europe and of Asia, but by no tribe in the north of North America. Many peoples have domesticated cattle, but there are still existent quite a number of peoples who have not done so. And of those who have done so, not all have

---

[1] The Andaman Island pygmies and the Bakango pygmies of the north-east Congo. See R. H. Lowie, "Cultural Anthropology," p. 55.
[2] Lowie, *op. cit.*, p. 41.

discovered all the uses to which cattle can be put; thus the Chinese have used cattle for traction, but they have not used them as food nor for dairy purposes.

Not only are there living contemporaneously peoples whose social heritage is that of Western civilization and peoples whose social heritage is comparable to that of our ancestors of the earlier Stone Ages, but also there are marked differences in social heritage between societies which are living at approximately the same level of technical achievement. Within the unity of what we call Western civilization there are many differences due to differences in social inheritance: differences in patterns of behaviour, differences in modes of thought. Thus some of the European nations have as an important part of their social heritage the tradition of the Roman Catholic Church, whilst others have the tradition of one or other of the Protestant Churches; and this means that there are marked differences in *ethos*. Again, the legal institutions of some of the European nations have been profoundly influenced by Roman law, whilst those of others have not been so influenced. And these are only some among the many differences due to different histories and therefore to different social heritages.

It is not only tribes and nations but every kind of society and sub-society which have their distinctive social heritage. Churches, colleges, professions, all of them have their traditional ways of thought and of action, their traditional sentiments and their traditional techniques. Regions also have them, and towns, and families. What these are depend upon their past histories, their contacts, the willingness or unwillingness of their neighbours to communicate new ideas, their own willingness or unwillingness to receive them.

It is to be noted that a great many persons may be affected by knowledge which is possessed by comparatively few of them. Of the hundreds of millions who use wireless and electricity and modern means of transport the vast majority could not explain the principles upon which the devices are based, still less could they reproduce those devices. It is

---

[1] Lowie, *op. cit.*, p. 41.

also often the case that only a small minority have a firm grasp of the principles by which a whole society is guided. The carriers of an important part of the social tradition may be few in proportion to those who live by it. There is always the possibility that the destruction of a key minority, or the acquisition by it of new ideas, may alter profoundly the life of a society.

Certainly it is true that whilst the social heritage is usually increasing in complexity and in content, there are many examples of recessions, when much of what has been handed down from the past has been lost. An outstanding example is the breakdown of the Roman civilization. It has been said that by the year A.D. 600 there was no one left in Europe who could have built one of the Roman aqueducts. Quite as striking as the decline in material techniques was the decline in the technique of government.

It should also be pointed out that whilst much which comes down to men in their social heritage is serviceable to them, this is by no means true of all of it; groups of men may inherit from the past cruel customs, ancient grudges, warped attitudes, paralysing inhibitions.

But on the whole the social heritages have been increasing social heritages, and probably they have been on the whole beneficial social heritages. It is seldom that the gains of the past are entirely lost; and stupid as men can be, they do profit by experience. Since writing and printing have been discovered, the means of preserving and of diffusing knowledge have been immensely augmented. Every library is a storehouse of information where it is possible at any time to find out what men of many lands and of many ages have learned and have thought about many subjects. To-day knowledge is so widely diffused that a complete loss of the more important techniques seems unlikely, though it is not impossible. One would like to think that the great humanitarian ideals and ethical codes, which have received some measure of acceptance over much of the world for many centuries, are also too firmly rooted and too widely diffused to perish.

*   *   *   *

It may be useful to conclude this chapter by comparing and contrasting heredity and social inheritance.

First of all, what each one gets by heredity is derived immediately from two persons only, and more remotely from not more than forty-eight stocks.[1] What each gets by social inheritance may be derived, and probably is derived, from many thousands of persons. A scholar has contact by books with thousands of dead men, and even those who are not scholars are influenced indirectly by the thoughts and emotions and acts of countless persons of past generations.

In the second place, our biologically given heritage comes to us at a moment in time, and what we receive then is unchangeable. The range of possible developments from it is wide, none the less it is a limited range. In the case of psychical transmission, there is no such definite, fateful moment, and there is no clear-cut division between the influence of the past and the influence of the present. Mind plays on mind during the whole of our lives, and impact may be from the mind of a contemporary or from the mind of a dead man. Whilst it is of great practical importance to distinguish between what is due to heredity and what is due to environment, there is no such need to distinguish sharply between psychical inheritance and psychical environment.

Lastly, and of immense importance, there is relatively small variability in that part of human life which depends upon heredity; the life histories of individuals have little effect upon the germplasm and consequently upon the heritage of the next generation. Such changes in societies as do arise from the operation of heredity are due to choices in mating and to differential fertilities. But the social heritage is a changing heritage, the history of each generation matters, and there may be rapid changes within a comparatively few years in what is transmitted. So far as stock is concerned, which means so far as physical and psychical potentialities at birth are concerned, the human race is probably not very different to-day from the human race of a thousand, or even

---

[1] Since there are 24 pairs of chromosomes in the human species. See Conklin, "Heredity and Environment," p. 318.

ten thousand, years ago. But because social heritage is cumulative, we are very different from the men of the past. And because of differences in their social heritages, contemporary societies composed of men of much the same stocks are very different from one another.

FURTHER READING

R. Briffault	.. ..	The Making of Humanity.
J. B. Bury	.. ..	History of Freedom of Thought.
R. H. Lowie	.. ..	Cultural Anthropology.
F. S. Marvin	.. ..	The Living Past.
Graham Wallas	.. ..	Our Social Heritage.
W. C. Dampier Whetham		History of Science.

CHAPTER VII

SOCIAL GROUPS

IN our first chapter we defined a society as *a number of persons whose lives affect one another substantially, together with their relationships and their set modes of thought and of behaviour.* Amongst such persons there will always be some who are distinguishable from the rest by some trait or traits which they have in common and which the others have not. Such persons constitute a group, and within any large society there are usually many groups. Not only are there many groups, but there are many bases of groupings, so that those who are in the same group in one respect may be in different groups in other respects. Thus two individuals of a society may be in the same religious group but be in different political groups, or they may belong to the same political group but be in different religious groups; or they may be of the same social class but be of different nationalities, or conversely they may be of the same nationality but be of different social class. In a complex society each individual is a member of many groups; the circles of these groups may overlap, but they do not as a rule coincide. In this country most, but not all, landowners are Conservatives in politics; some Conservatives are landowners, but there are many more who are not landowners; the two groups overlap but they do not coincide.

A social group in the widest sense is *a number of men and women having in common traits or circumstances which are, or which may be, significant for social life.* " Significant for social life " means that they are, or they may become, the bases of common consciousness, of common interests, and of common purposes. In our initial description of society we distinguished three levels of integration : (*a*) interaction, even if unwilled and unrecognized ; (*b*) mental interaction ; (*c*) willed relationships; and we agreed to speak of societies at these different levels as α-societies, β-societies, and γ-societies. So in the case of social groups we may classify them as (a) groups marked by similarity of traits or circumstances only; (b) groups in which similarity of traits or circumstances is recognized by their members, but has not yet given rise to organization; (c) groups in which similarity of traits or circumstances has produced both consciousness and organization. Following our usage with regard to societies, we will call these groups α-groups, β-groups, and γ-groups. With regard to the last of these we must note that sometimes it is society which imposes organization on such a basis rather than the group itself which organizes; e.g, the State in this and other countries both confers benefits, such as pensions, and enforces restrictions, such as retirement from office, on persons above certain ages. But there is not, as yet, any League of the Old or similar body, organized by the old to protect their interests.

Of our types of group the first is only potentially important; the members of it *may* become aware of what they have in common, *may* come to organize or come to be organized on the basis of common interests; but until they do so, the likeness between them usually affects society but little. It is hard to say when a common trait will become socially significant, or cease to be socially significant. It is only recently that we have become aware of the blood groups, but already they have social significance; donors of blood for transfusion are classified on that basis. It is not fantastic to conceive that in certain circumstances the members of the same blood group in an area might organize to safeguard their interests. That is to say that the blood group has already passed from being an α-group to being a rudimentary γ-group. And generally speaking, a group does not stay long at the second stage, it passes on to the third stage. At the second stage, and still more at the third stage, awareness of likenesses and of differences affects the behaviour of members of the group to one another, affects their behaviour to outsiders to the group, and affects the treatment of members of the group by outsiders to it. Group loyalties and conflicts between groups play a large part in human affairs.

Social groups are of many kinds and they may be classified in a large number of ways. One classification has already been suggested, and it should be noted that some sociologists reserve the term " group " for what we have called γ-groups, and that they apply to α-groups and to β-groups the term " quasi-group."[1] Another possible basis of classification is duration; a group may be in existence for a matter of minutes (as, for instance, a waiting crowd at a railway station), or for many centuries, as in the case of some churches and some empires. A third basis of classification is size; a group may consist of anything from two persons up to many millions of persons. Where the number of persons is small, and where frequent direct communication between them is possible, we have a primary or face to face group; where the number of persons is large, or where they are scattered, and communication must be by indirect means, we have what is called a secondary group. Thus the inhabitants of a village are a primary group; the inhabitants of a town are a secondary group. The growth of a primary group into a secondary group is usually a matter of great social significance, involving new kinds of relationship and necessitating more organization; failure to observe the transition may create serious difficulties, as is not infrequently seen when staffs of organizations expand rapidly.

A group (a) may comprise the whole population of a given area, or (b) it may be comprised in and be related to a given area, without constituting the whole population of that area; or (c) it may be without relationship to any particular area. As illustrations of these possibilities we may cite the English nation, the English Roman Catholics, the Roman Catholic Church. There is a further distinction which may be drawn, though it is usually difficult to make, between groups in whose case habitation of an area is a bond, but not the only bond (as, for instance, nations), and (d) groups whose essential

---

[1] See, for instance, Ginsberg's "Sociology," pp. 40-43. Rumney follows him, see " The Science of Society," p. 22.

nature is the relation of their members to a definite and distinctive territory. In this last case the group consists of those who share certain feelings, and perhaps certain ways of life, primarily because of such habitation. The inhabitants of Romney Marsh, or of the Forest of Dean, might perhaps be cited as forming groups of this kind.[1]

A further basis of classification is into groups with one function, or at most a few closely related functions, and groups which have no such limitation. M. Dékány has proposed the terms monotelic and polytelic.[2] Many propagandist bodies are monotelic; they exist for a single strictly defined purpose; the famous Anti-Corn Law League of the nineteenth century is a good example. By contrast a nation, a social class, or a family has no single purpose or single function; each of these is a polytelic group.

Closely allied to this distinction is that which may be made between groups arising spontaneously out of the circumstances of men's lives and groups which are the result of reflection and deliberate creation. Kinship groups and neighbourhood groups are examples of the former kind; it is almost inevitable that men should have traits, sentiments and interests in common with those who are related to them by blood, or who live in continual proximity to them. Such groups play a large part in the lives of all unsophisticated societies, a less but still important part in the societies of Western civilization. With them we contrast a typical propagandist or recreational group of modern times, such a body, let us say, as the British Institute of Adult Education, deliberately created by a small group of persons whose bond is a common enthusiasm.

Our last two dichotomies bear upon the distinction which has been drawn by many sociologists, notably MacIver, between *associations* and *communities*. The typical association is deliberately created for a single purpose or for a sharply limited number of closely related purposes. Community is

---

[1] The term "territorial group" is sometimes used, but there is considerable ambiguity attaching to it. I suggest that it should be reserved for the (*a*) groups. The (*b*) groups I should call "groups with a territorial reference." The (*d*) groups I should call "regional groups." But there is no convention in this matter.
[2] E. Dékány, "Communautés et Organisations."

a term much more difficult to define, and actually the accounts given of it by sociologists diverge considerably, but it would be generally agreed that communities arise spontaneously and that they are polytelic. Since community is a matter of degree, I have argued elsewhere[1] that the concept is better applied adjectivally than substantivally. Thus it is true to say that there is more of community among Roman Catholics than among Protestants, at least in this country, since Roman Catholic children are commonly segregated in education, Roman Catholic adults are discouraged from marriage outside their communion, and Roman Catholic participation in interdenominational effort is slight. Members of Protestant denominations are much less segregated, much less thrown upon the company of those of their own denomination, they do not have such close contact at so many points. But we should give a false impression if we said that the Roman Catholics formed a community whilst the Baptists or the Presbyterians were not a community. Actually there are few groups of any importance which do not develop some communal features; educational, political and propagandist bodies usually develop some social life, favouring the growth of multiple contacts and multiple relationships. I prefer, therefore, to say of groups that they are more or less communal, rather than that they are, or that they are not, communities.

Groups differ very much also in the extent to which membership of them is optional or not. There are many groups, especially in modern societies, of which membership is absolutely optional; it is for me to say whether I will, or will not, become a member of the Proportional Representation Society, or of the local tennis club. At the other extreme there are compulsions of two kinds, natural and social. To be a member of a family, or of a neighbourhood group, is a natural necessity, though there is considerable option as to how much one makes of that membership. To be a citizen of a State is usually a matter of social compulsion in the modern world; an option may, or may not, be given of

---

[1] See *Sociological Review*, January-April, 1940, "On Terminology."

changing one's citizenship. In many occupations there is social compulsion to join one's trade union or professional association. There are many intermediates between full option and full compulsion. Often social pressure is added to the pressure arising out of natural circumstances; thus, public opinion, to a very different extent in different societies, demands a recognition of kinship ties and of neighbourhood ties.

The actual groupings to be found, and their relative importance, have differed much in different societies. Groupings based on kinship play a big part in most primitive societies and also in some high civilizations, notably the Hindu civilization and the Chinese civilization. They count for a great deal less in Western civilization, especially since the industrial revolution. Family in some form is found everywhere and always; but clan and phratry and other large groups based on kinship have disappeared over a great part of the world. The larger family, that which includes several generations and collaterals, is still important in the East, where the head of a family is ruler over a considerable number of persons, and where each member has a claim upon the family resources in case of dire need, but it counts for comparatively little in this country to-day except among the aristocracy. The smaller family, parents and children, is here and almost everywhere a group of high importance. It is in it that children learn their first lessons in social life; it is through it that much of the social heritage is transmitted to them from the past; and family gives to the child its social status, though later on that social status may be altered. It is true that a number of functions have been transferred from the family and from the home to other groups and other places: the major part of formal education is given in the school, recreation is increasingly sought by members of the family as individuals, the family is only infrequently an occupational team. It is true that the authority of the parents is more sparingly used. But none the less the family remains a group of high cohesion, of great formative influence, and of great significance in the life of societies.

Other social groupings based on biological factors are those by age and by sex. In our own country to-day, and in a number of other countries, the State organizes certain services and requires certain duties on a basis of age; compulsory education, military service, and old age pensions are familiar examples. That is to say, society recognizes age groups and organizes on that basis. But there is as yet little organization of age groups by the members of them in their own interests; it is quite possible that this may develop. There are, it is true, Under Thirty Associations and Leagues of Youth and so on, but their importance is not great in the social fabric. But there are many peoples outside of Western civilization amongst whom age groups are well organized, and among whom members of the same age group have mutual responsibilities, and the group exercises discipline over its members.

The division into sexes counts for a great deal everywhere; men and women in most societies are assigned different rôles in such important matters as occupation, religion, and politics. There is often to be found some organization of themselves by men and by women to serve their different, and sometimes conflicting, interests; thus we have had in this country the Women's Suffrage Movement, and there are such bodies as the Open Door Council. But the amount of such organization is not great. There is a certain amount of group consciousness among and between the married and the unmarried, but it does not as a rule give rise to organization, at least in Western civilization. Such social devices as family allowances may, however, foster it, and we have recently experienced an agitation on the part of spinsters for pensions at an earlier age.

Other important groups, biologically based, are racial groups. When contacts are first made, or first become common, between men of markedly different physical appearance, there results, or there is heightened, a consciousness of likeness in those of each race and of unlikeness to those of the other race. The physical dissimilarity reinforces strongly that sense of otherness which is commonly felt at meetings of strangers. Should the contacts become frequent, there will be a process of habituation, so that the physical appearances no longer cause surprise and may cease to be noticed. But if, as is usually the case, cultural traits are also different, then physical differences will come to be associated with those cultural differences. The physical traits will also call to mind any behaviour in which a discrimination is made between individuals of the two races, especially behaviour which arouses strong emotion, such as aggression, domination, exploitation, expression of contempt. In such cases strong sentiments are likely to be formed, and the physical traits are likely to act as symbols able to rouse the sentiment into activity. When this is so, there are in existence two fully conscious racial groups.

If contacts persist and multiply, there may develop one of several situations. There may be after a time a deliberate segregation, contacts which cannot altogether be avoided being reduced to a minimum. This would appear to be the case in some parts of South East Europe, where villages occupied by inhabitants of different races are found in close propinquity but with restricted intercourse.[1] Or there may be established a symbiosis, each group finding within a new and enlarged society distinctive and complementary functions. Thus it is by no means uncommon to find certain occupations manned predominantly, perhaps entirely, by members of one racial group. Some such symbiosis seems to have existed formerly between Jews and Gentiles in Poland, the former being in the main the traders and professional men, whilst the latter were landowners or peasants. In such cases relationships may lack cordiality, but there need not be acute conflict. Or a situation may develop in which there is competition in the same spheres, with preferences actually or supposedly given by members of each racial group to their fellow members. In such circumstances there may be great bitterness. Or another type of situation may

---

[1] See Report of the International Commission (Carnegie Endowment) on the Causes and Conduct of the Balkan Wars, p. 134, *et al*. See also Max Handman, "Conflict and Equilibrium in a Border Area," in "Race and Culture Conflicts," ed., E. B. Reuter.

develop: there may be a process of assimilation, the two races and the two cultures blending.

In any case there is commonly a certain amount of miscegenation. In the worst conditions it results in the existence of a small number of usually unhappy individuals, who are either rejected or accepted very grudgingly by both parental groups. Sometimes it results in the formation of a new half-breed group, which develops its own consciousness and its own culture. Such are the Macanese, descendants of Portuguese and Chinese forefathers, and several other Eurasian groups. Sometimes there is complete fusion; in which case individuals exhibiting the characteristics of both the original types, and individuals exhibiting a blend of characters, will mix freely and on an equal footing, often with little consciousness of the wide physical differences between them. Such is the situation in Hawaii, where white men, yellow men, black men, and men of various other shades of colour are members of a single society, remarkably free from race prejudices and from race barriers. In our own country, and in most European countries, the situation is not fundamentally different, though the fusion was at a much earlier period. An inspection of any considerable assemblage of Englishmen will show a great diversity of physical types. Very different races have contributed to the making of our present population, but we are so familiar with the variety of physical types that few of us recognize how great that variety is.

It is by no means the case that common race must give rise to group consciousness or to group organization; it is only in certain situations that it does so. It is true, of course, that all the men of a race are an α-group; they have traits in common which *may* become socially significant. Of the great races of mankind, the white race may fairly be described as a β-group, since consciousness of membership of it is very widely diffused; but it is doubtful whether the yellow race or the black race can yet be so described. Certainly no one of the great races is organized on the basis of race; the white race as a whole does not yet constitute a γ-group, nor does the yellow race, nor does the black race. Some sub-races, and especially some half-breed groups of comparatively recent formation, come nearer to being γ-groups. But racial groups are almost always cultural groups as well, and they generally owe their distinctiveness far more to cultural differences than to differences of physical appearance, the importance of the latter being chiefly that they are pointers to the former. Much that is said and written about race as a basis of well-marked social groups is based on illusion, often of the nature of rationalizations. Racial myths, rather than racial realities, are forces in Europe to-day. But myths may operate very powerfully in human affairs.

Groupings based on neighbourhoods are very important in early stages of society, and are scarcely likely ever to become unimportant. Naturally, kinship groups and neighbourhood groups are often in large measure coincident, so that each basis of grouping reinforces the other. A small neighbourhood group of considerable importance in the mental development of each new generation is the play group, in which children commonly make their first acquaintance with a wider and more diversified society than that of the family. The populations of villages, towns, cities, are territorial groups whose nature depends in part on scale. The difference between a village and a town is that the population of the former is a face to face group, whilst the population of the latter is a secondary group; consequently more organization is needed to maintain social consciousness, and to express it, in the latter case than in the former case. In the case of great cities the scale presents problems of organization which are extremely difficult to solve. Special problems of group consciousness and of group organization present themselves in the case of conurbations and of mushroom growths, such as many of the new housing estates in this country. In both these cases the practical problem is to convert, if possible, α-groups into γ-groups.

Common occupation is another basis of grouping. Those who are engaged in the same kind of work are likely to have many traits and many circumstances in common. They have technical knowledge which outsiders to the occupation have not got. They work in settings of a particular type. Occupation sets its mark upon both bodies and minds. Men come to have a consciousness of their similarity arising out of common occupation, and of their dissimilarity from those in other occupations ; and those others have a corresponding consciousness. Commonly there is pride in their particular skill, and a sense of their contribution to social welfare. There are common economic interests. On the basis of common interests and of common sentiments organization usually arises. It takes different forms in different societies and at different times. In our time and in our country it takes the form of trade unions, of employers' associations, of professional associations. Such associations may or may not include all the members of the occupational group. Sometimes the organization is on an industrial basis rather than on an occupational basis, as in the case of some of the federations of trade unions and of the joint industrial councils. The purposes for which they exist are many : they include the protection of material interests, the admission and education of recruits to the occupation, the advancement of knowledge and of techniques, the formulation and enforcement of codes of ethics and of etiquettes, philanthropic and recreational provision.

There may be restrictions of various kinds on the composition of an occupational group. The nature of the occupation, and the conditions attaching to it, will attract some and repel others. There is often a sex discrimination : some occupations are reserved by law, custom, or the veto of the group to members of one sex only. Often there is class discrimination : certain occupations are supposed to be unsuited to persons of a certain social status. The cost of training and of entry, which may be raised artificially, debar many from many occupations.

As we have already seen, it is often the case that a social group has not a single basis, but several bases. Kinship groups are often neighbourhood groups also. So-called racial groups may often be described more truly as cultural groups. Racial groups and language groups often overlap, but seldom coincide. Because of these partial coincidences, because of the possibility of consciousness and organization on multiple bases, social groups may be very difficult to analyse and still more difficult to define. This is eminently true of two of the most important social groupings of modern times: social class and nation.

A social class is a group of persons conscious of certain common traits and of certain common ways of behaviour which distinguish them from members of other social classes with other traits and other ways of behaviour. Social intercourse is easy between members of the same social class, not easy and perhaps very difficult between members of different social classes. A distinctive feature of social class as a grouping is that it is hierarchical; members of each social class have a sense of deference due to them by members of some social classes and of deference due by them to members of other social classes. This is expressed by the use of terms which applied originally to space; we speak of upper, middle, lower classes. But we may also use qualitative terms and speak of " good " families, " better " social class; and there is undoubtedly some sense of comparative worth attaching to our estimates of social classes, though that worth is not moral worth.

The traits and the ways which mark off the members of one social class from those of another social class are of many kinds, and they are by no means the same always and everywhere. Commonly similarity in size of income is of importance; and, still more, similarity in distribution of expenditure. Kind of house and location of house are usually indications of social class, and so are quality and style of clothing. Certain occupations are supposed to be appropriate, or inappropriate, to certain social classes. Distinctive types of education are common, but by no means universal, accompaniments of class divisions. There are likely to be many subtle differences in manners, in bearing, in speech. Sometimes there are differences in moral codes. No one of these indications of social class is conclusive in itself, and it may be very misleading; it is the coincidence and cumulation of them which is to be taken as decisive. Many of the marks of social class are passed down as part of familial heritage, and it is therefore true in most societies that social class attaches primarily to families rather than to individuals; and that membership of a well-established and well-known family is an important, though not always a decisive, indication of social status.

To be a full member of a social class, an individual must both feel himself to be so and must be felt by others to be so. The ultimate tests are subjective. Useful objective criteria are easy exchange of hospitality and easy intermarriage, more especially the latter. The sharpness of the lines drawn between the social classes, the degree of deference expected and given, the possibilities of passing from one social class to another, differ widely in different societies. The origins of class divisions are many; they may derive from racial differences; they almost certainly result in in-breeding, so that there are likely to be, or to be accentuated, biological differences. They may derive from military conquest, or from political domination, or from diversity of religious beliefs or functions. They may derive from economic superiority; and where this is not the origin of class division, it is commonly achieved by the superior class. Economic advantage is the most common basis of class superiority in modern times, but it usually operates indirectly and with a time-lag which may extend to several generations.

It should be noted that social class, like several other common terms of sociology, is used in two senses. In the wider sense it covers all such hierarchical groups as have been described above. In the narrower sense it is used to denote such of them as are relatively fluid in contrast with "estates," which are defined and regulated by law, or "castes," which are strictly hereditary and between which mobility is negligible.

"Nation" is particularly hard to define. Nations are usually in some degree racial groups, in some degree territorial groups; but essentially they are cultural groups. They are racial groups in so far as their members are likely to be either predominantly of one race or, more likely still, products of a well-established mixture of races; and in so far as there is a consciousness of racial distinctiveness. But it should be observed that no nation coincides with a well-marked, homogeneous race, and these races are to be found in other nations also. They are territorial groups in the sense that they occupy exclusively certain areas, and about this soil and its features they commonly have very strong sentiments. But these sentiments are in large measure artificially induced, and they are at least as much products of nationhood as causes of it. In the main, nationhood depends upon the existence of distinctive sentiments arising out of a conjunction of cultural traits. Many and diverse cultural elements may be involved, few of them seem to be indispensable. Thus there may be a single distinctive language, but it is not necessary. There may be a common religion, but it is not necessary. Common social institutions are important, but nationhood is compatible with some degree of diversity. Common history plays a big part in strengthening national sentiment. What is indispensable is that there shall be a body of ideas shared by the great majority of members of the group. Thus Swiss nationhood is built on a passionate belief in local autonomy, a belief shared by citizens of all the cantons and overriding the differences in language, religion, and economic interests. Such ideas, and the behaviours to which they give rise, must be felt to be of such value that great sacrifices will be made, if necessary, to maintain their distinctiveness. Commonly in modern times this means that members of a nation wish to have their own State, or at the least a generous measure of self government.

It is not intended to attempt any further catalogue or even classification of the large number of groupings of many kinds which are to be found within societies. It is more relevant to our purpose to ask what are the main effects of the existence of groupings on the lives of men. In the first place, it is in and through groups that men co-operate; and the general effect of co-operation is to facilitate the business of living and to increase the reward to effort; though it is also true that a group may impose such unwise restrictions that an able individual may sometimes profit by a breakaway, and it is also true that membership of a group may make difficult or impossible co-operation with members of another group. In the second place, groups have in most cases a continuity of existence which bridges the generations, and it is in them and through them that the social heritage gets transmitted. In the third place, groups arise out of likenesses and differences between them, but also they emphasize and perpetuate those likenesses and differences by the imposition of the distinctive traditions which they elaborate. In the fourth place, participation in the life of the group is often itself a source of satisfaction to the individual; social intercourse is not merely a means to an end, it is an end in itself; moreover, the individual comes in the majority of cases to identify his interests in considerable measure with those of the group, and feels in doing so an extension and an exaltation of his personality. Lastly, groups are capable of growth to very large size, and when this is so, they produce human interactions on a scale and of a complexity which give them a very different character from the interactions of individuals or of small groups. In consequence a group may have a character just as an individual has a character. Whilst such a character is of course related to that of each component member of the group, it is not a simple relation and it is unsafe to argue from the character of the group to the character of its individual members or *vice versa*. It must be noted that the same individual may behave very differently in different relationships; and, to make the same point in another manner, there are often striking divergences in the behaviours of groups which are largely composed of the same men and women. The outstanding example of this is the low level of international morality as compared with commercial morality, or indeed with social morality in almost any other sphere.

FURTHER READING

L. L. Bernard	..	Introduction to Social Psychology.
G. D. H. Cole	..	Social Theory.
C. N. Cooley	..	Social Organization.
J. K. Folsom ..	..	The Family.
M. Ginsberg	..	Sociology.
Carlton Hayes	..	Essays on Nationalism.
R. M. MacIver	..	Community.
R. M. MacIver	..	The Modern State.
R. M. MacIver	..	Society.
ed. T. H. Marshall	..	Class Conflict.
T. H. Marshall	..	Social Class (in *Sociological Review*, Jan., 1934).
H. A. Mess ..	..	Social Groups in Modern England.
E. B. Reuter	..	Race Mixture.
J. H. Richardson	..	Industrial Relations in Great Britain.
Royal Institute of International Affairs		Nationalism.
R. H. Tawney	..	Equality.
E. Westermarck	..	A Short History of Human Marriage.

CHAPTER VIII

GOVERNMENT

Where a considerable number of persons live together in close social relationship, some means must be sought of harmonizing their interests and their wills and the actions which flow from them. Some actions must be forbidden, others may have to be demanded, others, again, can only be allowed upon conditions. Steps will have to be taken to coerce recalcitrant individuals or groups. Steps can also be taken, and devices can be employed, to mould the thinking and the feeling of individuals, so that compliance is easy and habitual. Further, common effort can produce or foster much that enhances the common welfare, so that there is a genuine coincidence of interests over wide spheres of life.

Formal and authoritative action to secure these ends is government; and the need for government and the problems of government arise in groups of many kinds; in a cricket club, in a church, in a trade union, as well as in a nation. Thus the English trade unions have made many experiments, which have been the subject of elaborate study by Mr. and Mrs. Sidney Webb. The differences between the Christian denominations are in part differences in mode of government. Constitutional questions occupy a good deal of the attention of organizers of voluntary societies of all kinds. The problems involved in harmonizing the interests and expressing the common will of members of groups are ubiquitous and perennial.

Since groups overlap, there are likely to be overlapping jurisdictions; and this we find to be the case. The same individual may be subjected to the rule and discipline of a church, of a trade union, of a town council, and of a national government, and to other rules and disciplines as well.

Naturally there is sometimes a conflict of authorities; history records many such. There is need, therefore, not only of regulation of the behaviour of individuals by the groups of which they are members, but also of the claims and behaviours of groups within a society. This need has been met in part, but in part only, by the evolution of States. " The modern State," writes Professor Laski, " is a territorial society, divided into Government and subjects, claiming within its allotted physical area a supremacy over all other institutions."[1]

The evolution of formal government, still more the evolution of States, has been a long and complicated process. In some primitive tribes to-day there is little of formal government, certainly nothing which can be said to correspond to the State. Yet the condition is far removed from anarchy. There are well-understood ways of doing things, and there are good reasons for compliance. Social habit, pressure of public opinion, fear of reciprocal action, and dread of supernatural powers, all act to keep men on the approved paths.

Formal government begins when specific functions are assigned to particular men, or to particular groups of men. One form it takes is the codification of rules, with specification of sanctions; many societies look back to a great lawgiver, and a number of early codes have come down to us. A second form of evolution is the appearance of judges, men supposed to be particularly conversant with the rules of the society and specially competent to interpret them in particular cases. A third form of evolution is the separation out of the whole society of a body of men to be lawgivers. And fourthly, there is the creation of executive bodies, and the endowment of one or more persons with authority to direct common activities of the members of the society.

There are many ways in which individuals and groups of individuals may come to be rulers in their societies. In the first place, experience counts for a good deal everywhere and, whether by formal rule or by mere prestige, elder men tend to govern. A measure of gerontocracy is widespread; it has

---

[1] The Grammar of Politics, p. 21.

given rise to such titles as alderman and senator and presbyter. In the second place, headship of a family, especially of the patriarchal family, is a form of governorship; and from that to headship of a clan is not a long step. Family structure and governmental structure are associated where the hereditary principle is observed. In the third place, there is prowess, especially in war. War demands able leadership and it demands strict subordination. Naturally the war leader acquires a claim to, and probably an appetite for, leadership in time of peace. Often, too, a group of successful invaders have imposed themselves as a ruling class upon a defeated native population. Fifthly, there are judges, men appointed to declare how the law applies in specific cases. Sixthly, there are medicine men and priests, those deemed to be skilful in handling supernatural powers. Seventhly, there are supposedly divine beings, or men in whom supernatural powers are supposed to be resident; this is one of the origins, if not the sole origin, of the institution of kingship. Eighthly, there are the rich; there are few societies in which the rich cannot make themselves felt. Finally, special abilities of many kinds, including ability to devise important new techniques, and including the gift of eloquence, may bring a man to authority. And authority may rest upon a combination of bases both at its inception and in its continuance.

Once authority has been established in a society a great many forces work to sustain it. Those who have tasted power will wish to continue to enjoy it, and to increase it. They will seek means of enhancing their prestige, and for that purpose ceremonial will be devised. The sanctions of religion will often be put behind authority. Those subordinated to authority will become habituated to their subordination. A body of sentiment will grow up round the institutions of government. Extensions may take place both of the territory over which a government claims authority and of the spheres of life of which it takes cognizance. There will probably be developments in the technique of government, and these will include the specialization and the hierarchisation of officials. There will be taxation in some form, certainly for the necessary expenses of government and probably as a form of exploitation.

The amount of government has differed very much in different societies. The extreme on the one hand is anarchy, which may exist for short periods in exceptional circumstances, such as the early days of a mining camp, or in the breakdown of accepted authority in revolutionary crises. At the other extreme is close and detailed prescription of conduct, and this has probably been pushed furthest in some small theocratic societies. In large societies the degree of control has depended considerably upon facilities of communication, but in part also upon dominant ideas. Thus in mediæval England with its abominable roads, a high degree of central control was not practicable; whilst in the earlier part of the nineteenth century the dominant philosophy of *laissez faire* would not permit it. In most of the nations of Western civilization in recent years both the will of governments to control and their ability to control have increased greatly. Modern science has placed a number of new instruments of power in the hands of governments: automobile, aeroplane, telephone, wireless, cheap and rapid printing and typing.

Rule may be by imposition on those governed, or it may be by their consent, or it may be by a mixture of both. Despotism is never entirely independent of public opinion; democracy is an ideal to which there can be approximation, but which can never be reached. But until modern times government has rarely depended upon the formal assent of the governed. Usually it has been in the hands of a privileged class, and commonly they have used their power to serve their own interests. So much has this been so that some writers[1] have considered States to have their origin and rationale as organs of exploitation of a dominant class. It ignores the considerable elements of consent of the governed which are to be found in many cases, and the identification by them of their interests with those of the State. It ignores also the services which even a bad government renders in the maintenance of order, and it ignores the extent to which rulers may

---

[1] E.g., F. Oppenheimer, "The State," and it is the common assumption of the whole Marxist school.

be moved either by genuine altruism or by vocational pride to improve the conditions of those over whom they rule.

We have spoken of the evolution of governments and also of the evolution of States. The two are not synonymous; the latter is a much later development than the former. In earlier stages of society government may develop to a large extent independently in various spheres of life, and this state of affairs continues far down history. Kinship groups, such as the clan, discipline their own members in many matters; so also do territorial communities such as villages and towns; occupational groups may do the same; the churches have their own rules and sanctions. Between all these forms of government there is likely to be some co-ordination, formal or informal, but there are abundant opportunities for conflict. It is only gradually that one set of rulers, and one set of institutions, whose primary function is the maintenance of some kind of security, begin to take precedence over all competitors. They claim a monopoly of the use of physical coercion; and they claim the function, very necessary in a complex society, of defining the limits and regulating the inter-relations of the other organs of government. When this concentration of power has taken place, the State may be said to have been established. Note the points in Professor Laski's definition, previously quoted:[1] the modern State claims the obedience of all persons living within a defined territory, and it claims supremacy over all other institutions.

This does not necessarily mean that the State directs all other forms and organs of government within its society. Churches claim that their authority is not derived from the State. Similar claims are often made for universities, for the press, for professional and occupational associations. The validity of such claims is a matter for social philosophy, and we shall not discuss it here. But we note as a matter of fact that there is a social philosophy which asserts it and there is a social philosophy which denies it. The former social philosophy is that of the democratic countries, which regard

---

[1] See p. 91.

with mistrust and with dislike the concentration of power; whilst in totalitarian countries the philosophy and the aim of their rulers demand full subordination of all organs of government to the State. It is relevant here to emphasize the importance of distinguishing between (*a*) the society co-terminous with the State; (*b*) the State, which is the supreme, but not the only organ of government of that society; (*c*) the Government, which is the group of persons actually handling the powers of the State at any particular time. Obviously, the legitimate claim of the three upon the loyalty of citizens is of a descending order. But it is a common device of rulers to confound the three.

A State claims supremacy over all persons, associations and institutions within its territory. There still remains a need to regulate relationships between States. Sometimes there is federation of States on equal terms, sometimes there is subordination of States to an imperial power. These federations, these empires, are sovereign States, as also are such States as have no permanent association with or subordination to another State; such sovereign States are not at present subject to any higher authority, though the relations between them are not entirely unregulated. There has grown up a body of international law. International law has been defined as *the rules which determine the conduct of the general body of civilized states in their mutual dealings*;[1] rules rather than law, for they depend upon voluntary assent, and there is at present no body charged with the duty of enforcing them. It does not follow that they are worthless. Some of the conventions are generally observed; and with regard to a number of others, the existence of standards has some effect on conduct. But it is of course very clear that the existence of a number of powerful sovereign States is fraught with danger in the modern world. The idea of a World State, with authority and with power to enforce at least a minimum of order, has emerged and it must be reckoned an idea-force.

---

[1] T. J. Lawrence, Principles of International Law, p. 1.

FURTHER READING

A. S. Diamond	Primitive Law.
L. T. Hobhouse	Social Development.
H. J. Laski	The Grammar of Politics.
T. J. Lawrence	Principles of International Law.
R. M. MacIver	The Modern State.
F. Oppenheimer	The State.

CHAPTER IX

RELIGION AND THE CHURCHES

EVERYWHERE and always the majority of men have been stirred by consciousness of great and mysterious powers at work in the world in which they live their lives, and everywhere and always they have tried in some way to achieve satisfactory relationships with those powers. How they have conceived them has differed much. Sometimes they have thought of them as impersonal; sometimes they have thought of them as being a number of separate and perhaps conflicting beings; and at a comparatively late period there emerged the idea of one supreme being, creator and ruler of all that exists. Sometimes these supernatural beings have been thought of as malevolent, sometimes as benevolent, most often as capricious. Sometimes men have sought to control these powers for personal, and perhaps anti-social, ends; that way lies magic. Sometimes they have sought to understand and to obey that which they felt to be wiser and better than themselves, and that road led to the great world religions. But magic and religion are not easily disentangled, and magical elements have persisted in all religions.

A developed religion consists of a number of elements. In the first place there are specific emotional attitudes of the believers towards the supernatural beings in whom they believe: awe, trust, gratitude, contrition, fear, love. In the second place, there is a body of ideas, including as a rule a cosmogony and an ethic. In the third place there are observances which both express and induce those emotions and those ideas. In the fourth place there is an organization of the believers for the purposes of their religious life.

It is comparatively easy to describe the externals of religion, but it is very difficult to assess its real hold upon men and its real effects upon society. But clearly it matters much to men and to society what fundamental attitudes are inculcated; whether, for instance, men derive from it an optimistic or a pessimistic attitude to life, whether it tends to make them scared or confident, active or supine. And clearly the nature of the ethical code embedded in a religion is a matter of great social consequence; thus, it has meant much to mankind that the higher religions have inculcated active and universal benevolence. Moreover, in most developed religions the two are not distinct but are blended; the attitude to the supernatural powers is associated with the attitude of men to men, and a code of social behaviour is taken to be an intrinsic part of the will of God.

What tends to happen is that the sanctions of religion are placed behind the *mores* of a society, to which also they have contributed heavily.[1] In general, if the *mores* are reasonably well adapted to the needs of that society in its time and situation, this reinforcement of them strengthens the society and enhances its welfare. But religion may add its tremendous strength to bad practices, and it is easy enough to frame a tremendous indictment against it on that score. On the other hand the development of higher moralities has been largely, though by no means entirely, a product of the religious spirit.

Religious life has produced its own organization, its own functionaries. From an early period some men (more rarely women) have been noted among their fellows as having special aptitude for dealing with sacred things. The priest is he who can most safely and most skilfully approach the awful powers; he mediates between them and his fellows; he regulates the ritual which must be observed. Obviously, the priest is a powerful person in a believing society. And, just as other men, he is likely to enjoy power and he will be tempted to

---

[1] The relationship is well illustrated in such a code as that contained in Deuteronomy xii to xxvi. Parts of the code relate to religious observances, e.g., regulations as to sacrifices, food and clothing taboos; see, for instance xvii, 1, xiv, 12-19, xxii, 11. Other parts of the code enjoin generous behaviour, e.g., to widows and to aliens, and represent the best ethical elements in the Judaism of the period; see, for instance, xxiv, 19-22. Yet other parts of it are social regulations, e.g., with regard to property, whose justification is utilitarian and whose origin is probably secular; see, for instance, xxi, 15-17, xxiii, 24-25.

abuse his power. With the passing of time and the development of religion a professional priesthood is likely to be established with its hierarchies, though there are great religions, notably Islam, in which priesthood plays a very small part.

Another typical figure of religion is the prophet, the man who claims to be charged with a message from the supernatural world. In primitive societies many kinds of abnormal experiences may be taken as evidence of inspiration, and the prophet is frequently a neuropath. The utterances of prophets range from the wild ravings of deranged persons to the sane and lofty deliverances of such men as Isaiah. Among the prophets are to be counted the founders of religions. Whilst a prophet may give a conservative and even a reactionary message, yet typically the prophet is an innovator. In contrast to the priest his office is not easily professionalized. It may to a limited extent be institutionalized; the prophet was a recognized figure with a recognized function in the religious life of Israel.

Another group of functionaries are the exponents of the creed and holy writings and of their corollaries. Such were the scribes in the time of Christ, the ecclesiastical lawyers in mediæval Christianity, the casuists and the theologians of our own or any other time. Close akin to these are the teachers. To them is entrusted the formulation, the development, and the presentation of the intellectual elements in religion. Such men may have a considerable influence, especially in a society whose government has theocratic elements. Thus, over most of Christendom the regulation of marriage was in the hands of ecclesiastical lawyers down to recent times.

In many societies there is special recognition of sainthood, of the fact, that is, that some men exhibit in a high degree the qualities characteristic of the form of religion which they profess. Sainthood may be manifested in many ways, some of which do not at all commend themselves to the modern Western man. None the less it may be sainthood in another society; and if that society is deeply religious, sainthood may give considerable influence in secular affairs. The career of

Mahatma Gandhi is a contemporary illustration. Akin to sainthood, at a rather lower level, is the segregation of men and women in religious orders living according to a rule which usually imposes a measure of asceticism.

Certain features are to be found in the cults of most religions. There are holy places, holy seasons, holy writings. Of holy persons we have already spoken. All these offer facilities for communication with the supernatural powers; they are generally conceived also as offering dangers to those who misuse them. Believers worship at the appointed seasons in the appointed places under the direction of appointed persons. The worship includes hymns and prayers, often sacrifices and sacraments, and it commonly follows a ritual, that is to say a set order, which is itself regarded as having a certain sacredness.

In relation to society the various elements in a cult have both primary and secondary importances. The primary importance of a cult is the expression it gives to emotions and the association of those emotions with a body of ideas and of practices. And the rites not only express, but also impress the emotions and the associated ideas. It is almost impossible to conceive of a religion persisting without a considerable element of ritual. In particular, the association of rites with the great occasions of life both strengthens the hold of religion upon the adherent and underlines the significance of the happening. The secondary importance of the cult derives from the nature of its rites and practices; they may be gross or refined, cruel or kindly, linked or unlinked to ethical thought and behaviour; and their nature will affect the nature of the worshippers. And they may modify profoundly social life in other than religious aspects. Thus, the institution of fasts and of festivals has repercussions on economic life. And such a widespread practice as the celibacy of priests and of members of religious orders clearly affects both quantity and quality of population.

The union of believers in a religion is a Church in its associational aspect; the body of practices and of relationships by which they seek to achieve their purposes is a Church in its institutional aspect. Some kind of a Church is to be found wherever there is religion, but fully developed and closely organized Churches are more rare; indeed, there is no complete parallel to be found elsewhere to the Churches of Christendom. The functions of a Church are the regulation of the cult, the propagation of the religion, the maintenance of discipline. Every Church is of necessity an instrument of social control; it seeks to ensure some measure of conformity, at least amongst its members, possibly in the larger society if the two are not coincident. There are many methods which it may employ; it may issue pronouncements, it may impose penances, it may excommunicate, it will certainly engender a strong public opinion, it may be charged with the teaching of the young, it may resort to physical coercion. Above all and characteristically, it controls by virtue of an acknowledged claim to special knowledge of, and influence with, supernatural powers.

Churches make great claims upon the allegiance of men, and so do States. Inevitably there must be an attempt made to adjust their respective claims. Such adjustments have been of many kinds, and they have not been made without much friction. One type of adjustment is that of theocracy, where the Church is the State and its officers exercise the functions of secular government. Pure theocracies have been rare in the world's history; more commonly a powerful Church has allowed and has used a subservient State. At the other extreme is complete control of the Church by the State, generally known in the modern Western world as Erastianism. There are many intermediate positions. A Church may be established, that is to say that its function of maintaining religion may receive express recognition by the State. The State may or may not contribute to its expenses. There may be co-establishment, the recognition by the State of several Churches as playing a legitimate and necessary part in society; it may or it may not contribute to their funds. Or a State may profess secularism, permitting but not assisting Church activities; and the secularism may be more or less benevolent or hostile. It may even attempt to proscribe organized religion, as Soviet Russia did for a few years. There are many variants and combinations of these attitudes possible. And apart from formal relationships there may be informal understandings; where both State and Church offer positions of great influence and possibly of great emolument, they are likely to be occupied by men drawn from the same social stratum, and having many ideas in common.

The Churches, therefore, are to be regarded in one aspect as instruments of social control; they tend to produce similarity of ideas and conformity of behaviour. Normally their requirements are in harmony with those of the State, though they may ask their adherents to go two miles where the State only asks them to go one mile. But there may be conflicts of outlook; the moralities demanded by Church and by State may diverge; different Churches may demand different moralities within the same State. Such divergences are very apparent to-day in a number of countries of Western civilization in regard to sexual relations. In such cases acute tensions may develop. And those who hold office in both Churches and States are apt to be suspicious of divided loyalties. That again receives notable illustration to-day in Germany and elsewhere. Finally, a live religion usually contains radical elements as well as conservative elements. For all these reasons, whilst religion is usually, and in the main, a powerful integrating force in a society, it may also in certain circumstances be disruptive.

FURTHER READING

A. S. Diamond	Primitive Law.
W. Dibelius	England.
ed. K. Grubb	The Church and the State.
L. T. Hobhouse	Morals in Evolution.
E. A. Ross	Social Control.

CHAPTER X

EDUCATION

INTO the complicated societies of mankind there are continually being born new individuals who have almost everything to learn; almost everything, because specific instincts play a comparatively small part in human life and social heritage plays a very great part. The new individuals have to receive the social heritage of their society, or at least a part of it; and in doing so their own lives should be enriched and also they should be adapted to life in that society. This acquisition of the social heritage by the new individual is education in the widest sense of that term. It includes a good deal of absorption of knowledge and of attitudes from the life around him, a process which is facilitated by man's innate powers of memorising and of generalizing, powers which of course do not appear at once, but which develop during childhood, and which may be very much strengthened by appropriate training. But absorption from the environment is only a small part of education; measures are taken by the older generation to facilitate the process, so that education includes a good deal of teaching and of being taught. Much of this teaching is informal and casual, but there is also formal education, which in modern societies is usually given by a specialized class of men and women, teachers by profession. In the narrower sense, formal education is the deliberate and planned direction of influences on the young, and the deliberate transmission to them of part of the social heritage of their society.

What is transmitted? The reader should refer back to what was said in a previous chapter about social heritage. Education, both formal and informal, is much concerned with the acquisition of techniques. Some simple lessons in adaptation to environment must be learned by every member of a society; it is, for instance, essential that every person growing up in our society should learn to avoid traffic dangers, whilst in tropical countries the child must learn early to avoid over exposure to sunlight. There will be in most societies techniques which, though they may not be vitally necessary, are highly desirable, and are taught to all; thus in the majority of the countries of Western civilization everyone is now taught to read and to write. But also in all but the most primitive societies, and eminently in Western civilization, there is elaborate specialization of functions and many techniques are learned by some only, and it may be by very few.

In the second place there is the teaching and learning of what might perhaps be called techniques, but what are perhaps better distinguished as the vehicles of knowledge, languages and terminologies. The choice of language or languages in which instruction shall be given is a matter of great importance, both because it determines the range of information to which there is access and also because strong sentiments attach to words and to combinations of words. Familiarity with a particular language and with a particular literature is an important element in the sentiment of nationality, and education is therefore a powerful instrument in the creation and maintenance of national feeling.

In the next place the developing members of a society acquire the ideas, the sentiments, the attitudes, and the ways of behaviour which are current in that society. To a large extent this is the result of informal education, but in most societies resort is had to formal education also. Thus there will be dogmatic teaching about religion and about morality, and this may be given by parent, by priest, or by teacher. Probably also some view will be given of the structure and of the functioning of the society. To illustrate from a pre-literate society, Dr. Meek tells us that among the Ibo the children are taught by their parents to be punctilious in the correct use of the terms applied to family relationships, family being a wider and more complicated group than that which goes by the name among us.[1] They are also taken round farms and shown how to demarcate boundaries.[2] And amongst the Ibos, as in most pre-literate societies, much use is made of ritual to impress ideas.

In literate societies, where formal education is more developed, ritual still plays some part; the scholars may participate in national or local celebrations, the national anthem will be sung, the mayor of the town may visit them in pomp. But the part played by ritual is smaller than it is in primitive societies, and more reliance is placed upon books and the verbal lesson. Some knowledge of the structure of society is given, though to a large extent in an indirect form, and in the teaching of history, of geography, and of literature; perhaps in the case of elder children in the teaching of economics and of civics. But it may be doubted whether in this, and in a number of other countries of our complicated Western civilization, the majority of citizens acquire a clear idea of the social structure; indeed it seems likely that in this respect they are less adequately educated than are many pre-literate peoples.

Education can also facilitate the transmission to members of the new generation of ideas, sentiments, attitudes, and habits. To a considerable extent this is done informally, much of it at home or in the small neighbourhood group; some of it is the informal and casual accompaniment of formal education; much more of it is the informal, but by no means unpurposed, accompaniment of formal education; and some of it is a direct subject of formal education. In these various ways, differently proportioned in different spheres and in different societies, the new generation is assimilated to its predecessors in such matters as religion, patriotism, social stratification, sex behaviour, and in countless other matters great and small.

In view of the importance of the educational process within society it is not surprising that there has been much competition for its control. The chief claimants have been the family,

---
[1] C. K. Meek, "Law and Authority in a Nigerian Tribe," p. 299.
[2] *Op cit.*, p. 298.

the church, and the state. In modern times the tension has been particularly acute between churches and states. Where there is not one church, but several competing churches with conflicting ideas within a single State, the position is still more difficult. Similarly there may be groups with conflicting political ideals, or with conflicting cultures, within a single State. In all such cases the control of education is a matter as to which the groups, religious or political or cultural, cannot be indifferent. Many forms of compromise are to be found.

Among the claimants to a share in control are the teachers. Naturally they are willing to work within a general framework approved by society, but they demand for themselves a considerable discretion as to the methods and the content of education and some freedom of expression on matters as to which different views may be held. In this country university teachers are particularly jealous of their freedom to teach what they believe to be true, and the universities claim a high degree of autonomy. This freedom of the teachers is precarious everywhere, and is denied in many countries.

There is yet another claimant to a voice in the direction of education, and that is the child himself. Naturally the child cannot urge the claim; it is made on his behalf. It has received serious attention in educational circles in our own time, and the administration of it has given rise to a number of experiments and to a number of modifications of methods.

For whilst we can consider education as an instrument of social control, a process of shaping members of the new generation to the requirements of society, we can also consider education from the standpoint of the welfare of the individual scholar. Each child has unique potentialities, each has his own desires and his own ambitions, each will have to play an individual rôle in society. Body and mind can be brought to high efficiency, personality can be enriched, facilities can be afforded for self-expression, he or she can be equipped to face the inevitable competition of life. In an individualistic and highly competitive society education will often be regarded by teachers, and still more by parents, as preparation for a career, and scholars will naturally adopt the same view. " The world's mine oyster, which I with sword will open." Teachers, parents, the child himself, will co-operate to see that the sword is as sharp as possible.

These two aims of education are not to be conceived of as mutually exclusive nor as necessarily opposed. Personality is usually enriched, and efficiency is usually enhanced by adjustment to the society in which the individual will have to live it; and society is the better for having members who are sharply individualized. The mutual adjustments of societies and of their component individuals may take many forms, and education will be partly determinant of, partly determined by, the prevalent form of adjustment in any particular society.

The claim raised on behalf of the child raises another question, a kindred question, and that is the extent to which education proceeds by indoctrination. By indoctrination is meant that ideas are conveyed to the child in such a form and in such an emotional setting that they are not only received uncritically, which is to a considerable extent unavoidable in the early years, but that they will remain highly resistant to any later impacts which might change them. At the other extreme to indoctrination is the induction in a scholar of a critical attitude, so that he will seek for himself, and not necessarily take on trust, both information and ideas. Inevitably all education must contain some indoctrination, but the line of division is according to whether the teachers do or do not aim at the ultimate emergence of a mind free to question.

Societies differ widely in respect of the education which is given in them, and are differentiated by it. Not only do they differ in aims and in methods and in control, they also differ with regard to the conditions of access. The amount and quality of education which a child will receive may be determined on the basis of its abilities, on the basis of the wealth and social status of its parents, and perhaps according to the political and religious views of its parents. In this country at the present time all children receive some education; exceptional ability may secure a long and good education for the child of poor parents; a special type of school is maintained for the children of the upper classes; and there are schools of special types to meet the wishes of members of particular religious bodies. There is no discrimination on political grounds in this country, but in some countries of Europe only those are admitted to study at universities who hold views acceptable to the government.

Those who control and those who practise education have tremendous power in their hands to mould a new generation; but it is important to recognize that there are limits set to what they can accomplish. There are, first of all, the limitations set by the material. No amount of effort can make a silk purse out of a sow's ear, nor can the most skilful education make a really efficient man out of a dull wit. It is probably true also, for our comfort, that so diverse are men's gifts, and so powerful is the urge in some to experiment, that it is in point of fact difficult for even the most tyrannous church or state to crush out all spontaneity and all diversity. In the other direction there is a check upon rapidity of change inherent in the very continuity of life. No one has assessed the transforming power of education more highly than Benjamin Kidd, who, in a famous passage, wrote:

" Give us the Young. Give us the Young, and we will create a new mind and a new earth in a single generation."[1]

But who are the " we " to whom the children are to be given? If they are typical of the older generation, they will have been shaped by the same social heritage as it. And if they are not typical of their generation, it is improbable that the young will be handed over to their moulding. Teachers would in any case find themselves restrained by authority, should they attempt to impose ideals far removed from those prevalent in the society of which they are part. What is true is that, as recent events in Europe have demonstrated strikingly, a small number of men with strong views, who have gained control of the organization of education, can impress those views rapidly and effectively upon a large part of the younger generation. In that sense Kidd's dictum is justified.

---

[1] B. Kidd, " The Science of Power," p. 298.

FURTHER READING

W. Boyd	..	History of Education.
W. Dibelius	..	England.
C. A. Ellwood	..	Introduction to Social Psychology.
J. L. Gray	..	The Nation's Intelligence.
W. D. Hambly	..	Origins of Education amongst Primitive Peoples.
B. Kidd	..	The Science of Power.
H. A. Mess	..	Social Groups in Modern England.
E. A. Ross	..	Social Control.
F. Smith	..	History of Elementary Education.
R. H. Tawney	..	Equality.

CHAPTER XI

THE GEOGRAPHICAL SETTING

THE lives of men, like those of all other creatures, are conditioned by their physical environments; but in their case the conditioning is both more complicated and less rigid than in the case of the lower creation, because of their psychic endowment. It is more complicated, because many of the effects of their surroundings are very indirect, as for instance in their influence on the formation of such composite sentiments as patriotism; it is more complicated also because the geographical setting is itself being modified continually by human action. It is less rigid, because in the first place man is an animal tolerant of a wide variety of conditions, and because in the second place the mental powers of men both enable them to increase their natural adaptability and also to make big changes in their environments. Thus it comes about that the geographical settings in which men live their lives are only in part natural data; in part they are of men's making. They or their predecessors have made tracks and roads, perhaps canals and tunnels; they have embanked and drained and irrigated; they have hewn down forests and they have planted; they have levelled, they have mined, and they have quarried. Or, at least, they may have done any of these things; pretty certainly they will have done some of them. The physical settings of men's lives are therefore in considerable measure artefact, and the landscapes on which men gaze are mostly cultural landscapes.[1]

Between men and their surroundings there is therefore a continuous interaction. There are fundamental geographical conditions which remain constant over immensely long periods

---

[1] See "Man's Adaptation of Nature: Studies of the Cultural Landscape," by P. W. Bryan.

of time; the generations pass, but the mountains and the seas remain. But even with regard to these unchanging features the response of men to the pressures they exert differs very much from age to age and from society to society, according to technological level, social institutions, and the enterprise or lack of enterprise of a population. During many millennia the Atlantic Ocean sundered the two hemispheres; within the last few centuries it has provided routes between them. Palm Beach and Miami are what they are partly in virtue of their situation and of their climate, but partly because the social institutions of the United States allow the existence of a very wealthy leisured class. Tyre and Sidon were great seaports in their day, not merely or mainly in virtue of their geographical situation, but because the Phœnicians were enterprising and daring.

In the study of the relationships between geographical conditions and the structures and the natures of societies there are few generalizations which are of much value; the profitable course is to study the effects of particular settings upon particular societies at a particular period. It is, however, possible to indicate some types of interaction.

Thus, the nature of any society is conditioned by its location, since this will have an obvious bearing upon the contacts which it is likely to make. In our day of easy communications the factor of propinquity is of less importance than formerly, and societies may be influenced profoundly by distant societies of which they would have had little or no knowledge a few centuries ago. Yet even to-day the location of a society makes some contacts inevitable and others more or less likely. The political thought of the Swedes and of the Finns is bound to be affected by the nearness of their countries to Germany and to Russia. The political thought of the United States, of Japan, of China, and of Australia, is affected by their common proximity to the Pacific Ocean.

Mere linear distance is of less importance than accessibility, of which it is only one factor; accessibility depends partly upon natural features and partly upon the facilities for transport which men have organized. It is common experience that a town lying off a main traffic route may be less accessible, more isolated, than a town lying at a much greater distance along that route. Little pockets of relatively inaccessible country are often to be found close to great cities.[1] The question of accessibility or of isolation bears profoundly on the nature of societies. Easy communication makes possible interaction of many kinds; it fosters contacts of cultures and interplay of thought. It tends to break down mere custom. It makes possible centralized government, a closely integrated society, a homogeneity of culture over wide areas. Isolation, on the contrary, favours conservatism and distinctiveness; those who live in remote areas are not aware, or are not so aware, of what men think and of what men do in other areas. Districts difficult of access have often sheltered defeated groups, enabling them to preserve their identity, their own ways of life, and sometimes their political liberty.

In the second place many towns owe their origin to some advantage of location, to their being at the terminal points of important routes or at the points of intersection of important routes, or to their being at spots where rivers could be bridged or forded, or at eminences above flood level, or in the neighbourhood of an exceptionally good water supply. The reasons which determine the growth of the town are likely to influence its nature as a society. Thus at the meeting points of long distance routes men of different cultures are likely to have dealings with one another, and there is at least the possibility of mutual stimulation and of some minds being set free from the narrow ways of thought of a particular society.

The nature of the soil has its reactions upon the societies which live upon it; it imposes limits to the size and to the density of the population which can live on a given area at any particular technological level; and the size and density of populations affect the nature of societies. In general the larger and the denser the population the more regulation there

---

[1] E.g., to illustrate from our own land, the countryside of north Essex is still remarkably little affected by nearness to London; some of the small industrial settlements on the south bank of the Tyne have had very slight contacts with the neighbouring city of Newcastle.

is likely to be; primary groups are likely to be of less importance relatively to secondary groups, and the ties of kinship and of neighbourhood are likely to be relatively less strong and cultural ties relatively more strong. Where minerals occur, there is likely to be brought into existence at some period a highly specialized population; there is likelihood also of the settlement being of a transitory nature owing to the progressive exhaustion of the minerals.

Climate, of which the most important elements are range of temperatures, degree of humidity, and prevalent winds, is commonly held to act directly upon societies as stimulant or depressant of human energies, but exact and detailed knowledge on this subject is remarkably scanty. A distinction needs to be drawn between the operation of climate upon native populations and upon recent immigrants. In extreme climates high civilizations are scarcely likely to develop, and in the most extreme climates human existence is a virtuosity. Climate affects social life indirectly through the vegetation, and still more indirectly through the fauna which that vegetation can support. The patriarchal family, if it was not an inevitable product of the steppe, was at least well adapted to the life of pastoral peoples on the steppes.

It is not difficult to catalogue a very large number of ways in which geographical conditions influence the lives of men and therefore influence the nature of the societies of which men are members. They influence the kind of house built, the kind of food eaten, the amount and the style of clothing, the occupations of men. They influence religious ideas, partly by colouring the forms of myths and partly by the degree of difficulty which they impose in the matter of making a livelihood. "Europe was saved by climate from the dogma of the world-illusion,"[1] says one writer, and he expresses epigrammatically the truth that philosophies which evade the hard facts of life are more easily conceived and more easily accepted where the bare necessities of life are few and are obtainable without great labour.

---

[1] H. C. Tracey, "Towards the Open," pp. 187-88.

Geographical settings influence societies also by the sentiments to which they give rise. The elements in scenery have a powerful effect upon a human spirit; round them, especially if they are the surroundings of childhood, almost ineradicable sentiments grow. Love of scenery is a strong ingredient in both local and national patriotisms. Perceptions and appreciations of landscapes are much heightened by the work of artists and of writers, men and women of unusually keen sensibilities and with a gift of communicating to others what they themselves experience. Village, countryside, or city become more vivid to their inhabitants when they have seen a painting of it, or have read a description of it, or have heard it lauded in an oration. Sometimes there is a deliberate, and even competitive, writing up of a district. Certainly the champions of nationalism have been ready to use the artist and the writer for propagandist purposes.

But, clearly, national sentiments, and many other territorial sentiments, could not arise of themselves out of geographical conditions. Spontaneous sentiments of any strength would only be generated for most men in respect of the country within a few miles of their homes, and in so far as these sentiments were common to a group, it would probably be a primary group. A few travellers might form sentiments with regard to wider areas; and, as we are all travellers nowadays, the region with regard to which we might form sentiments of any strength would be considerably wider than in former days. But the sentiments arising out of geographical features could not by themselves develop into an English sentiment or a French sentiment. There are many kinds of scenery in England and in France, and even within a county or a department, there may be a wide variety. The emotions aroused by these different kinds of scenery are in many men incorporated in one powerful sentiment: they think of English scenery, of Sussex scenery. This is only possible because they have a conception of England, a conception of Sussex; the various landscapes could not of themselves create a conception of England, or even of Sussex. They could at most contribute to it; we must look elsewhere, or at least for other elements, to explain why England and English landscape, or Sussex and Sussex landscape, seem to have a unity. And so it is with other countries.

The explanation is in part at least that when a well-knit society, and, in particular, when a nation-state occupies a definite area, it sets its marks upon that area. The landscapes which men see are cultural landscapes, and each nation has its distinctive culture; its system of land tenure, its social stratification, its religious institutions and its educational institutions, its political structure, all of these set their marks upon its landscapes. England would look different if it had peasant proprietorship, or if it were a Roman Catholic country, or if less scope were given to local authorities. Moreover, those artists and writers, who heighten so much our perceptions, have themselves the sentiment of nationality and of smaller district. Thus whilst sentiments attaching to the geographical setting heighten patriotism they also derive from patriotism.

Geographical facts condition social life, but they do not determine it; there are few generalizations to be made of wide validity. They offer as a rule a multiplicity of possibilities from which a choice may be made. A population living by a seashore may, or may not, become a seafaring population. A site suitable for a city may, or may not, be utilized. Mineral wealth may be exploited, or it may be left unexploited for many centuries. Different peoples make different uses of the same kind of territories; the same people makes different uses of the same territory at different times. The most that can be said is that geographical conditions make certain forms of human activity possible, perhaps likely, whilst they make other forms of human activity unlikely, perhaps impossible.

Finally, men are increasingly able to master their physical environments. Cultural adaptation of natural data can be carried much further to-day than ever before. High explosives, the internal combustion engine, and the caterpillar tractor have made it less necessary than formerly to keep to ancient routes. Even the desert, the most formidable of all barriers, is ceasing to isolate. Whilst geographical features are still of importance, and obviously will always be of importance, their constraints are less imperative and less direct than formerly.

FURTHER READING

J. Brunhes	Human Geography.
L. Febvre	A Geographical Introduction to History.
E. C. Hayes	Introduction to the Study of Sociology, Chapter III.
Ellsworth Huntington	Civilization and Climate.
P. Sorokin	Contemporary Sociological Theories, Chapters II and III.

CHAPTER XII

SUMMARY AND CONCLUSION

FROM a biological standpoint human life may be thought of as a continual weaving and reweaving of bundles of threads, an infinite variety of patterns on a limited number of themes. Sometimes threads are damaged or bad, and a pattern will be spoilt. Sometimes threads disappear altogether; more seldom new threads appear, by what process is still obscure. Heredity determines the range of characteristics and of capabilities which can be exhibited by individuals, and consequently by groups; it will depend upon environment and upon the contingencies of history which of the possibilities in the range are realized. A European society, a Japanese society, a Negro society will differ in some respects because of differences in racial composition. With regard to physical features this is obvious; it is probably true also, though it is not so obvious and the differences are largely unexplored, with regard to psychical features. And it is quite likely that some of the psychical differences between European societies are due to differences in racial composition. Such differences may also account in part for differences in physical or psychical characteristics between groups of many kinds within the greater societies, e.g., differences between social classes, between religious groups, between small local groups. But because stocks have been so much mixed, and because it is so difficult to distinguish hereditary factors from environmental factors, generalizations about racial qualities should be received cautiously in the present state of knowledge. The evidence at present available suggests that the mental and temperamental endowments of the different races do not differ very widely. On the other hand the range of differences of individuals within races and within most societies is wide and is of great importance.

The biological composition of a group may be altered by fresh contacts and by intermarriages (or matings outside of marriage) with members of other groups; and this alteration in biological composition may take place whilst the language and the social structure of the original group persist little changed. In the United States of America, for instance, language and social institutions are predominantly Anglo-Saxon, far more so than are the racial elements in the population. The opposite may occur; an alien language and an alien social structure may be imposed upon or be adopted by a population whose racial composition changes little. In considerable measure this has been the story of the Highlands of Scotland.

Differential fertility may alter the relative proportions between groups. Thus, in the nineteenth century the white races increased more rapidly than the other races of the world. Differential fertility may alter the relative proportions of groups within a society. Thus, in England the Roman Catholics have a much higher birth rate than those of other religious sects, and for this reason (there may be other reasons also) they are at present an increasing proportion of the population. Differential fertility may raise or lower the quality of the stock of a society; the increase in the proportion of mentally defective persons in this country gives us reason to fear that we are breeding disproportionately from inferior stocks. But here again the great difficulty of distinguishing between hereditary factors and environmental factors needs to be borne in mind. The one sure test of badness of stock is failure of several generations of individuals to respond to improvements in environment.

From the psychological standpoint we have to think of the energy of life as flowing along channels whose outlines are more or less clearly defined, more or less constant, channels which are sometimes laid down in the hereditary pattern and sometimes the product of social pressures. As to the more and the less, as to what is fixed by heredity and what can vary according to environment, there is still much uncertainty, and widely different opinions are expressed by psychologists. That the forms of expression of human energy can be more varied than can be those of the energies of the lower animals, that they owe less to heredity and more to environment, is recognized by all. But we do not yet know within what limits the forms of expression can be varied, and we do not yet know in which cases there is a specificity which is inborn and therefore ineradicable. In short, we do not know what are the limits to the plasticity of human nature. There is probably no other point at which the progress of sociology is so sharply halted for want of knowledge.

It is scarcely to be doubted that the inborn specific urges differ in their relative strengths in individuals of different stocks; and it may be that there are significant differences in this respect between different races, but as to this also our knowledge is very slight. What is certainly true is that some of the specific urges are immensely powerful and are coercive to an extent which few realize. The nature of these urges is often hidden from the conscious mind; perceptions are often modified, and reason is often perverted, to serve their ends; it is important to realize the part which dissociation and rationalization play in mental life. Human reason, biologically late in development, is weak and fallible; none the less it is the distinctive feature in human societies. Temperament is physiologically and in the main hereditarily determined, but it may be modified by environmental forces; and the same is true of that sum of energies which we call vitality.

Ideas and feelings organize themselves in the human mind in sentiments; and in terms of sentiments a great deal of social behaviour can be described. We all recognize the power of such sentiments as love of family, love of nation, attachment to church, class feeling, and such violent aversions as anti-Semitism, anti-clericalism. The history of nations, the history of churches, and much other social history, is in one aspect the history of the growth, transformation, and decay of collective sentiments. In these sentiments two elements are to be distinguished: intellectual concepts and emotional associations. Ideas, more or less consciously formulated, such as the ideas of liberty, justice, toleration, have played a great part in shaping the behaviour of men. But so also have dimly recognized or quite unrecognized associations of feelings with persons, objects, or ideas. We have all met blind loyalty to a leader, sentimental attachments to houses or to scenery, and unthinking responses to symbols or to catchwords.

Man is distinguished from the animals amongst other things by his capacity to store knowledge and to transmit it. In contrast, therefore, to the animals, man has a cumulative social heritage: there are transmitted to each generation from previous generations customs, sentiments, ideas and ideals, and techniques of many kinds. It is largely because of this cumulative social heritage that human life differs so much at different periods of time, and that there is such a thing as human history in a sense in which there is not animal history.

Whether man is innately gregarious or not is disputed; but, however that may be, the facts of long helpless immaturity, of powers of communication with his fellows, and of power to form concepts, have combined to make him a creature which constructs societies and is moulded by the societies of his making. Every man is a member of many groups; each group is what it is by reason of the nature of the individuals composing it, by reason of its structure and history, and by reason of the purposes and sentiments which animate it; and, reciprocally, the individuals composing it are other than they would be if they did not participate in the life of that group. Men to-day live in a complex network of groupings. The earliest groups in the history of mankind, the earliest groups in the life of each individual, must of necessity be based on kinship and neighbourhood. But progressively, both for the individual in his lifetime and for the human race in history, groups are psychically rather than physically determined. Social class, religious sect, political party, nation, come to play a larger part; family and neighbourhood group, though never ceasing to be important, count relatively less.

The complexity of the social relationships necessitates

mutual adaptations both of individuals and of groups, and these are not always easily made and certainly they are not always made spontaneously. Every group, therefore, adopts measures, persuasive or coercive, to secure that such adaptations shall be made. To this end there have been evolved a number of methods of social control; they are employed by many groups and agents of groups, and especially by states, churches, schools and professional associations. There is also the ill-defined, but often overwhelming, pressure of public opinion.

Lastly in this brief review of the forces shaping human societies, there is their external environment, the geographical setting. Location, topography, climate, natural resources, have played a great part in the past and must always do so. They have exercised pressures, they have offered possibilities and they have denied other possibilities; but they have not determined the nature of societies, and men have responded very differently at different times to the opportunities and challenges presented to them. As men have become increasingly able to modify their physical environments, the direct effects of these upon societies has become relatively less.

* * * *

In the foregoing paragraphs, and in the preceding chapters of this book, our task has been one of analysis. And for such a purpose it is legitimate and necessary to isolate factors and to try to trace the operation of each one. And quite often we are able to say, with more or less plausibility, that such and such a factor accounts for such and such a feature. But whenever we make such a statement we ought to be on our guard; and, in so far as we are true sociologists, we shall be watching for the interaction of many factors, and we shall be aware of the difficulties of distinguishing what is due to one and what is due to another. It is one of the marks of a society that there is such interaction, that each component is likely to be adapted in some measure to every other component. It is a sound canon of study that societies should be considered holistically.

The interdependence of parts in a society was perceived by Auguste Comte, the founder of sociology, who spoke of it as the "consensus." "There must always be a spontaneous harmony between the whole and the parts of the social system, the elements of which must inevitably be, sooner or later, combined in a mode entirely conformable to their nature."[1] Comte, pioneering, made many statements which later sociologists have been compelled to qualify. The qualification necessary to this statement is that "later" may be very much later. Indeed, one may doubt whether the statement is of universal validity. There is indeed a continuous tendency to a harmony of the different elements in a society; there is a necessity for some kind of accommodation to one another; but it is also true that discordant elements may co-exist within a society and may persist for a very long time. In human societies, as elsewhere in nature, we have to do with partial autonomies and with imperfect harmonies.

We proceed now to illustrate the interactions of different factors in social life. In the first place there are interactions between factors of the same kind. Thus, whilst it is probably true that each gene has a predominant part in determining some character of a human being, it is also true that a gene does not operate in isolation from the other genes. On the contrary, the mode of its operation is very much affected by the nature of the other genes with which it is in association, and the whole body of genes is to each individual gene an environment conditioning its action.[2] If again we make our examination in the range of psychological factors, we find here also a partial autonomy and an imperfect harmony; men are driven by urges which may be in conflict—the literature of psycho-analysis provides abundance of illustrations—but in most of us some tolerable accommodation is arrived at, the personality is more or less satisfactorily integrated. So it is with ideas; it is perfectly true that human beings have a remarkable capacity for entertaining ideas which are fundamentally disharmonious, but it is true also that ideas are

---

[1] Auguste Comte, "Positive Philosophy," (ed. Martineau), pp. 78-79.
[2] See E. B. Ford, "Mendelism and Evolution," pp. 34-41.

brought into relation with one another in the minds of most men, and that some kind of philosophy of life is usually formed.

All these are illustrations of partial autonomies and of imperfect harmonies within the lives of individuals; but equally, and more directly relevant to our subject, are the partial autonomies and the imperfect harmonies to be discerned in collective life. Thus there will be conflicting philosophies found within the same society, and these may reflect and exacerbate struggles between groups within that society; but unless the state of that society is pathological in high degree, and the society is in danger of disintegration, there will be a substratum of agreement, a body of ideas, a philosophy, common to the great majority of the members of that society, expressing and confirming their unity. So it is also with customs, usages, and social institutions; there may co-exist in any society the strangest seeming incompatibles. But also there is likely to be interaction between these customs, usages, social institutions; they tend to be accommodated to one another, and if one changes it is likely that others will change too.

We proceed now to illustrate interactions between the different factors in social life. In the first place we note that the genetic composition of a society is likely to be affected by its geographical setting; obviously this determines to a large extent the contacts which are likely to be made and consequently the marriages which are likely to take place. The choice of mates is also affected by ideas and by sentiments; thus the strong sentiments attaching to social class narrow it, as also the strong views and feelings attaching to religion may do. Such views and such sentiments may be re-enforced by law; thus, some of the American states penalise racial miscegenation. *Per contra*, it is possible (and some sociologists would say that it is certain) that the genetic composition of a society may affect its attitudes, its modes of behaviour, and its social institutions.

The complex relationships between ideas and social behaviour have been discussed in a previous chapter, where it was insisted that the relationships were reciprocal: ideas affect social behaviour, but also social behaviour affects ideas. If ideas change, social institutions are likely to change, and *vice versa*. But again the correspondence is imperfect. Ideas may long be prevalent in a society, they may even be officially endorsed, whilst there are social institutions which are in contradiction to them.[1] Christianity has been the official religion in nearly all European countries for periods ranging from eight hundred to sixteen hundred years, but he would be a bold man who asserted that the major social institutions of Europe were accommodated even approximately to the teachings of Christianity. The American Declaration of Independence of 1776 included a statement that all men are created equal, but slavery was a recognized American institution for another ninety years. These discrepancies are the themes of satirists and of reformers, whose writings and efforts do sometimes bring about either a change of practices or a change of ideas, or both, and thus lessen the extent of disharmony.

Enough illustrations have been given of our present theme, that any factor in a society may interact with any other factor, that there is a tendency towards harmony, that some degree of harmony must be achieved if the society is to continue to exist, but that glaring disharmonies may exist for a long time; in short, that in every society there is exhibited a partial autonomy of its parts and an imperfect harmony between them.

* * * *

In conclusion we may ask what we gain by such an analysis as we have attempted in this book. We should gain by an increased appreciation of the forces which make our lives what they are, and which make our societies what they are. This book will have failed of one of its purposes if it has not made its readers realize, or realize more clearly, the extent to which our thoughts and feelings and actions are the result of forces at work, of which we are only partly conscious and which

---

[1] Margaret Mead writes: "Tchambuli institutions and the emphases of their society are, to a certain extent, at odds with one another." "Sex and Temperament in Three Primitive Societies," p. 307.

we can only partly control. First of all, there is heredity; we are what we are, in large measure, by virtue of our parentage. We did not determine that we should be men of such and such kind. It is no doing of ours which has caused us to be white men and not black men or yellow men, or indeed men at all. It is no merit of ours if we happen to have good brains, and no demerit if our brains are poor. And it is no doing of ours if by nature we are quick-tempered or placid. Up to a point our lives have been determined for us. Nature dealt the cards, and we have to play them. Nor is that all. Given that particular heredity, we might have developed in many different ways. But it was not left to us alone to settle which of the many possibilities of our nature should be realized. A number of other persons influenced us more or less deliberately: parents, neighbours, teachers, preachers, legislators, and all of these have contributed to make us what we are. Our parentage gave us, not only a certain physical heredity, but also a certain social heritage. We learned to speak the English language, we learned English history, and read English literature; particular ways of looking at things, particular likes and dislikes were early implanted in us, just as other men were moulded by a French or German or Chinese upbringing. We have caught many customs from our elders and from our neighbours and we shall follow them all our lives. And if we should be inclined to deviate widely, to strike out new lines for ourselves, society will have something to say about it: there are all sorts of fences and obstacles for those who wander too far from the beaten tracks. There are many things the law will not allow us to do; there are some things which it will insist on our doing. And even when the law is silent, there is public opinion to reckon with. There is a steady pressure on us from first to last to conform within fairly narrow limits to recognized and accepted patterns of living. It is only gradually and partially that we come to recognize this shaping of our lives. Of the forces which shape us, some are external to the individual; for instance, the constraint of law. Others are written in our own natures as, for instance, the strength of inborn urges. Some of the forces, heredity, for example, set sharp and final limits to what is possible for us; other forces, such as public opinion, press upon us gently at times and at other times almost irresistibly.

But whilst we are not as free as the unsophisticated think, it is by no means the case that we are slaves of forces which we are unable to influence. Our lives are moulded but they are not determined. A living creature is seldom entirely passive; it has some power of choice, some power of varying its response; and the higher the creature is in the scale of life, the more it can choose among the various possibilities of its nature and of its circumstances. Our heredity does indeed determine much about our lives; but it is part of that heredity, part of the human nature which it has given us, that we can become aware of our own make-up and can exercise a choice within the range of possibilities given us. We have to accept as data the urges which are born in us, or early induced in us, but we can often choose between different ways of giving them expression. And so it is with regard to social heritage, all the knowledge and ideas and attitude to life and way of living which have come to us because we were born into a particular society. We cannot escape from it—probably we should not wish to escape from it—but we can become aware of the peculiar quality of it, and we can make an intelligent use of it. Institutions shape our behaviour; but institutions were made by men and they can be changed by men. Custom and public opinion set heavy hands upon us; but we can question the value of any particular custom; and we are part of public opinion. We are swayed by powerful leadership; but we can be good followers without being blind followers. And it is open to us to give a lead as well as to take a lead; there is no one without some small sphere in which his influence counts.

Our lives are rough hewn by the forces which we have been describing, but they are finally shaped by us. And the more we are aware of the moulding forces, the less we need be mere products of their pressures. In the realm of physical science man has enlarged his powers as he has learned the laws from which he cannot escape: it is since he has known the law of gravitation that he has learned to fly. And so, too, with regard to mind and emotions, it is by learning the laws to which they are subject that we are likely to achieve greater freedom. It is one of the hopeful things in the world to-day that there is an increasing number of men and women who have some understanding of the forces by which their lives are shaped, and who are thereby delivered from mere slavery to them. Men by their intellectual powers have achieved much mastery of inanimate nature and of the lower creation. They are now beginning to apply those intellectual powers to systematic and scientific exploration of their own natures and behaviour. Inevitably this means a study of the nature of society, since men cannot live except as members of societies. These comparatively new studies are beset with great difficulties; their development marks a new and hopeful phase in the history of mankind.

FURTHER READING

Ruth Benedict .. .. Patterns of Culture.

M. Ginsberg .. .. Sociology.

R. M. MacIver .. .. The Elements of Social Science.

R. M. MacIver .. .. Society.

P. Sorokin .. .. Contemporary Sociological Theories.

NAME INDEX

Alverdes, F., 65n.
Amos, 67
Aristotle, 45, 67, 69
Arnold, M., 59

Bacon, Roger, 68
Bakunin, M., 62n.
Bartlett, F. C., 24n.
Beaglehole, E., 51
Beethoven, L. von, 25
Benedict, Ruth, 22
Brown, J. F., 32n.
Bryan, P. W., 110n.

Carr, E. H., 64
Comte, A., 122
Conklin, E. G., 17n., 72n.

Dante, 25
Dékány, E., 77n.
Dewey, J., 33n.
Dickinson, G. L., 42
Durkheim, E., 12, 57, 58

Ellwood, C. A., 39n.

Fleming, R. M., 28n.
Ford, E. B., 122n.
Fouillée, A., 60

Gandhi, G. K., 100
Garth, T. R., 23n., 24
Gates, R. Ruggles, 17n., 28n.
Gautama, 67
Ginsberg, M., 12n., 33n., 47, 76n.
Gobineau, M. A. de, 23n.

Handman, M., 81n.
Hart, B., 35, 36
Hegel, G. W. F., 62n.
Hogben, L. T., 26n.

Isaiah, 63n., 67

Joel, 63n.
Jones, D. Caradog, 29n.

Kidd, B., 108

Lange, J., 28n.
Lao Tze, 67
Laski, H. J., 91, 94
Lawrence, T. J., 95n.
Lidbetter, E. J., 29n.
Lowie, R. H., 69n., 70

MacIver, R. M., 12n., 77
McDougall, W. G., 22n., 33n., 39n.
Marx, K., 62n., 64, 93n.
Mead, M., 124n.
Meek, C. K., 104, 105n.
Mendel, G., 15, 16, 58n.
Micah, 63n.
Mosca, G., 61n.

Nadel, S. F., 24n.

Oppenheimer, F., 93n.

Proudhon, P. J., 53

Rumney, J., 76n.

Sinclair, Upton, 41
Smith, J. A., 62n.
Socrates, 67
Sorokin, P., 33n.
Sumner, W. G., 43n., 45

Titian, 25
Tracey, W. C., 113n.

Voltaire, 42

Wallas, Graham, 12
Webb, S. & B., 90
Weber, M., 64
Wells, H. G., 42
Westermarck, E., 43, 49
Woodworth, R. S., 32, 33n.
Woolf, L., 63n.

Young, Arthur, 52

Zechariah, 63n.

SUBJECT INDEX

Acquired characters, 18, 29
Age groups, 80
Alpine race, 21, 22
Associations, 77,
Australoid race, 21

Bequest, 53, 61
Blood groups, 75

Capitalism, 48
Caucasian race, 21
Christianity, Christendom, 27, 50, 99, 124
Chromosomes, 15, 16, 18, 72n.
Churches, 10, 45, 48, 50, 70, 94, 106, 119, 121, and Chapter IX passim.
Class, Social, 9, 24, 26, 27, 85, 86, 108, 117, 120
Climate, 113, 121
Communities, 77, 78
Complexes, 35
Conurbations, 12
Conventions, 54, 58
Customs, 11, 41, 42, 43, 46, 49, 66, 120, 125, 126

Dissociation, 37, 119
Dominance, 17, 18

Education, Chapter X
Environment, 104, 117, 118, 119, and Chapter II passim.
Ethos, 59, 70

Family, 26, 44, 45, 46, 49, 55, 77, 78, 79, 86, 92, 105, 113, 119, 120
Feudal system, 10, 47, 48, 61

Genes, 15, 16, 17, 122
Geographical environment, 11, 27, 121, 123, and Chapter XI
Government, 10, 112, and Chapter VIII

Heredity, 66, 117, 118, 125, and Chapter II passim.
Heritage, Social, 26, 103, 108, 120, 125, 126, and Chapter VI

Ideas, 66, 104, 105, 119, 120, 122, 123, 124, 126, and Chapter V.
Idea-Force, 60, 95
Ideology, 61
Imitation, 39
Inbreeding, 27, 28
Indoctrination, 107
Inheritance, 52, 53
Institutions, Social, 10, 11, 44, 45, 46, 47, 48, 49, 50, 51, 52, 60, 61, 66, 91, 100, 111, 123, 124, 126
Intellect, Intelligence, 24, 25, 26

Kinship, 77, 79, 83, 84, 94, 113
Kingship, 45, 92

Language, 87, 118
Law, 27, 46, 54, 58, 95, 125
Linkage, 18, 20
Location, 111, 112, 121

Marriage, 44, 45, 46, 49, 50, 51, 118, 123
Mediterranean race, 21, 22
Miscegenation, 28, 82, 123
Morals, 58, 102, 104
Mores, 58, 59, 98

Nation, nationalism, 86, 87, 114, 115, 119, 120
Negroes, 21, 22, 24
Neighbourhood group, 83, 84, 105, 120
Nordic race, 21, 22
Nutrition, 21

Occupational groups, 83, 84
Outbreeding, 27, 28

Patriotism, 114, 115
Population, 112, 113
Priest, priesthood, 45, 48, 92, 98, 99
Primogeniture, 10, 45
Property, 45, 47, 49, 51, 52, 53, 60
Protestants, 36, 70, 78

SUBJECT INDEX—continued

Race, 21, 22, 23, 24, 28, 80, 81, 82, 84, 86, 117, 119
Rationalization, 36, 60, 83, 119
Reason, 38, 119
Recessivity, 17, 18, 19, 27, 28
Religion, 27, 46, 52, 59, 92, 104, 105, 113, 117, 120, and Chapter IX
Roman Catholics, 8, 36, 70, 76, 118

Sentiments, 27, 35, 36, 37, 38, 39, 46, 65, 66, 81, 87, 104, 105, 110, 114, 115, 119, 120, 123

Sex differences, 25, 31, 80
Slavery, 27, 44, 45, 46, 49, 54, 55
State, 45, 48, 50, 78, 82, 91, 94, 95, 101, 106, 108, 115, 121

Techniques, 21, 40, 66, 71, 104
Temperament, 24, 28, 119

Unit characters, 16, 21
Usages, 11, 43, 44, 47, 50, 66, 123

War, 9, 45, 46, 49, 53, 54, 92